I0434937

Spatial Patterns of Land Cover in the United States

A Technical Document Supporting the Forest Service 2010 RPA Assessment

Kurt H. Riitters

The Author:

Kurt H. Riitters, Research Ecologist, U.S. Department of
Agriculture Forest Service, Southern Research Station, Eastern Forest
Environmental Threat Assessment Center, 3041 Cornwallis Road,
Research Triangle Park, NC 27709,

Product Disclaimer

The use of trade or firm names in this publication is for reader information and does not
imply endorsement by the U.S. Department of Agriculture of any product or service.

April 2011

Southern Research Station
200 W. T. Weaver Blvd.
Ashville, NC 28804

Spatial Patterns of Land Cover in the United States: A Technical Document Supporting the Forest Service 2010 RPA Assessment

Kurt H. Riitters

Contents

List of Tables

List of Figures

Spatial Patterns of Land Cover in the United States: A Technical Document Supporting the Forest Service 2010 RPA Assessment

Kurt H. Riitters

Abstract

Land cover patterns inventoried from a national land cover map provide information about the landscape context and fragmentation of the Nation's forests, grasslands, and shrublands. This inventory is required to quantify, map, and evaluate the capacities of landscapes to provide ecological goods and services sustainably. This report documents the procedures to inventory and summarize land cover composition, juxtaposition, and structure as exhibited at several measurement scales. National and regional results are summarized in tabular form, and representative statistics are illustrated in figures (for States) and maps (for counties). The baseline information in this inventory is a starting point for future analyses of landscape changes.

Keywords: Forest, fragmentation, grassland, inventory, land cover pattern, Resources Planning Act, shrubland.

INTRODUCTION

In 1974, the U.S. Congress called for an assessment of the Nation's renewable resources because reliable information was necessary to manage the resources properly and to inform policy decisions. This mandate is embodied in the Forest and Rangeland Renewable Resources Planning Act (RPA) of 1974, P.L. 93-378, 88 Stat. 475, as amended. The need for reliable information continues, as does the need for a broad perspective that considers the social, economic, and ecological aspects of natural resource conditions, ecosystem health, and sustainability. This report addresses the RPA requirement for "an inventory... of present and potential renewable resources, and an evaluation of opportunities for improving their yield of tangible and intangible services...." The RPA requires a U.S. Department of Agriculture assessment every 10 years. The 2010 RPA Assessment provides a snapshot of current U.S. forest and rangeland conditions and trends on all ownerships, identifies drivers of change, and projects conditions 50 years into the future. Included in the 2010 RPA Assessment are analyses of the status and trends of recreation, water, timber, wildlife, and range resources as well as land use change, climate change, and urban forestry.

The inventory statistics in this report were prepared to support the 2010 RPA Assessment. Many environmental processes are affected by, or depend on, the spatial arrangement of land cover. RPA land cover pattern assessments have focused solely on the role of pattern as a modifier of wildlife habitat quality, but land cover patterns are of interest for many other reasons. Society is informed of landscape changes through headline indicators of urban sprawl and forest fragmentation. In spatial ecology, the pattern-process hypothesis implies that many other ecological processes and biophysical phenomena depend on land cover patterns. Land cover patterns partly determine the available spectrum of recreation opportunities, and land-use planners often consider land cover patterns as they define "sense of place." Resource managers need to know where to manage what types of land cover in order to produce a desired balance of ecological goods and services.

There has been research on the specific causes or effects of land cover patterns in particular situations, but most of that information is either too limited in geographic extent or too detailed in ecological scope to form the basis of a national inventory of land cover patterns. Instead, a generic and extensible approach informed by specific research findings is required. A generic approach provides information that may be interpreted consistently across the Nation and in relation to more than one socio-ecological process or resource management question. An extensible approach retains flexibility, enabling users to expand or add to the capabilities of the information according to local requirements. For example, other research results could be used to interpret nationally consistent statistics in particular situations, perhaps by combining national maps of land cover patterns with more detailed maps of local conditions (Riitters and others 2003). A generic and extensible approach to an inventory of land cover patterns promotes integrated landscape management by enabling common usage of the same information across disciplines and locations (Riitters and others 2000). It also permits rigorous evaluations of the tradeoffs or synergies involved in land cover pattern management. In a top-down framework for resource management, a national inventory is suitable for regional and national applications and is not expected to answer local questions in detail.

The focus of this inventory is on land cover pattern itself, and not on pattern as a cause or consequence of some other environmental attribute. One reason is that information about pattern itself is needed to inform resource management questions about the current locations of different types of patterns, opportunities for restoring natural patterns, or mitigating effects caused by undesirable patterns. The second reason is that reliable measurement of pattern itself is prerequisite to interpreting the causes or consequences of pattern (Bogaert 2003). Apart from the specific consequences of pattern, the physical structure of land cover constrains a landscape's capacity to sustain ecological goods and services (Burkhard and others 2009, O'Neill and others 1997), and it may indicate future landscape transformations (Riitters and others 2009a). For example, the existence of agriculture juxtaposed with forest in a given landscape limits the capacity of that landscape to provide amenities associated with intact forest. While the presence of intact forest does not by itself guarantee that such amenities will be realized, the absence of intact forest certainly precludes their realization. A national inventory of land cover patterns helps in identifying constraints, opportunities, and tradeoffs for improving the yield of socio-ecological goods and services.

Previous national assessments of land cover patterns for the RPA focused solely on forest land cover. Those assessments indicated that forest was usually the dominant land cover type where it occurred and was typically close to other forest, but also that fragmentation was so pervasive that the majority of forest land was at risk from edge effects extending only 100 m from forest edge (Riitters and others 2002, 2004b). The importance of anthropogenic land use as a cause of fragmentation is clear in the pervasiveness of roads (Riitters and Wickham 2003) and in the concentration of the least-fragmented forest in public ownership (e.g., large parks and public forests) and remote locations (Heilman and others 2002, Riitters and others 2004a). The observed geographic variation in the proximate causes, types, and scales of fragmentation implies substantial geographic variation in the mechanisms of actual impacts from fragmentation (Riitters and Coulston 2005, Wade 2004, Wade and others 2003). For this report, the inventory of land cover patterns was extended to include the shrubland and grassland land cover types as well as new measures of landscape patterns not specific to one land cover type.

The primary data used for this report comes from a national land cover map (fig. 1), circa 2001, from the National Land Cover Database (NLCD) (Homer and others 2004, 2007). The NLCD map is a product of an ongoing Federal effort to map land cover and other biophysical attributes of the United States periodically, consistently, and across the Nation. An upcoming update of the NLCD for the year 2006 supports analysis of trends in a future RPA assessment.[1] Unlike a sample-based inventory or a compendium of local maps, a wall-to-wall national map such as the NLCD supports a complete census of land cover patterns in a consistent way nationwide.

NLCD definitions of land cover types may differ from other RPA definitions and, as a result, absolute area measurements from the NLCD map are not comparable to other RPA area estimates. To discourage such comparisons, the statistics in this report are expressed in terms of percentages of total areas as defined by the NLCD map. Sampling errors are not reported here because the inventory was a complete census. Land cover labeling errors on the NLCD map are translated to measurement errors when measuring patterns on that map.

This inventory used three basic pattern metrics to describe the spatial patterns and landscape context of forests, grasslands, and shrublands. The "area density" and "land cover structure" metrics are used to evaluate the occurrence of each of those land cover types in relation to itself (i.e., to each type), thereby describing attributes such as fragmentation, dominance, edge abundance, and patchiness. A third metric called "landscape mosaic" is used to evaluate the juxtaposition of anthropogenic and natural land cover, thereby describing the landscape context within which those three land cover types were found, e.g., the context of a forest-urban interface. Each measurement was taken at several measurement scales for the following reasons: land cover patterns are naturally scale-dependent; there is no optimum measurement scale; and patterns as exhibited at different measurement scales are all potentially meaningful. In addition, how a given pattern metric changes with measurement scale may also be interpreted with respect to a different aspect of pattern (Riitters 2005) or the range of scales over which certain types of patterns exist (Zurlini and others 2007). Statistics derived from the three metrics were then summarized nationally and by RPA region (fig. 2), with examples shown by State and by county (fig. 3).

---

[1] Wickham and others (2008) assessed temporal trends of forest patterns by using forest maps derived from the 1992 and 2001 NLCD maps, but those maps are not strictly comparable to the original 2001 NLCD land cover map that is used here.

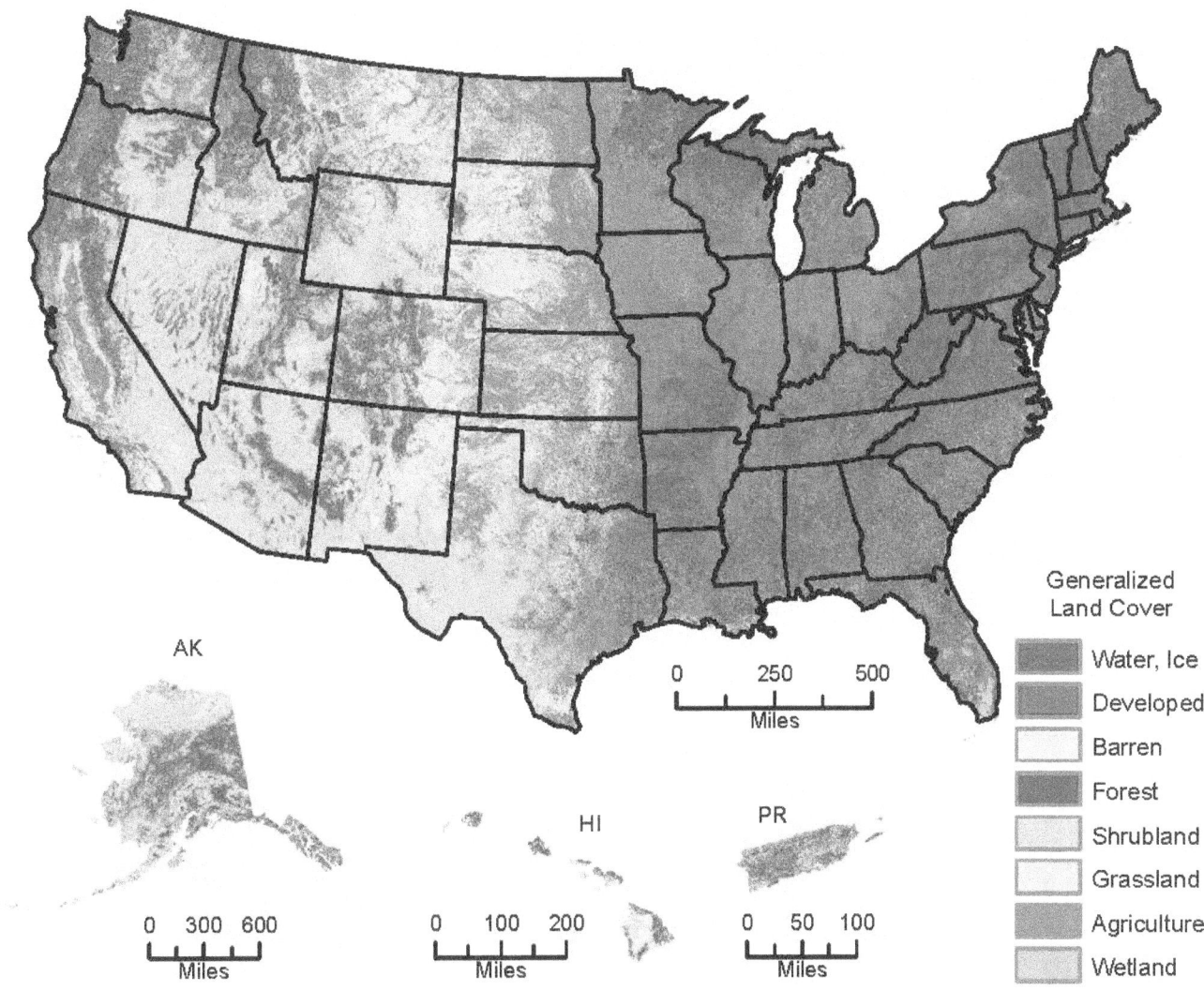

Figure 1—Generalized land cover map of the United States, 2001.

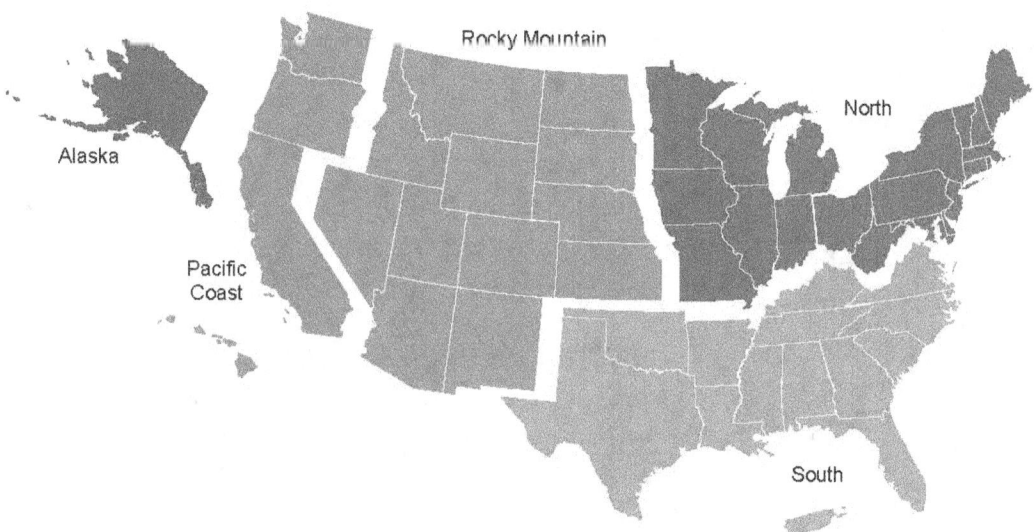

Figure 2—Five Forest and Rangeland Renewable Resources Planning Act (RPA) assessment regions used to summarize land cover pattern metrics.

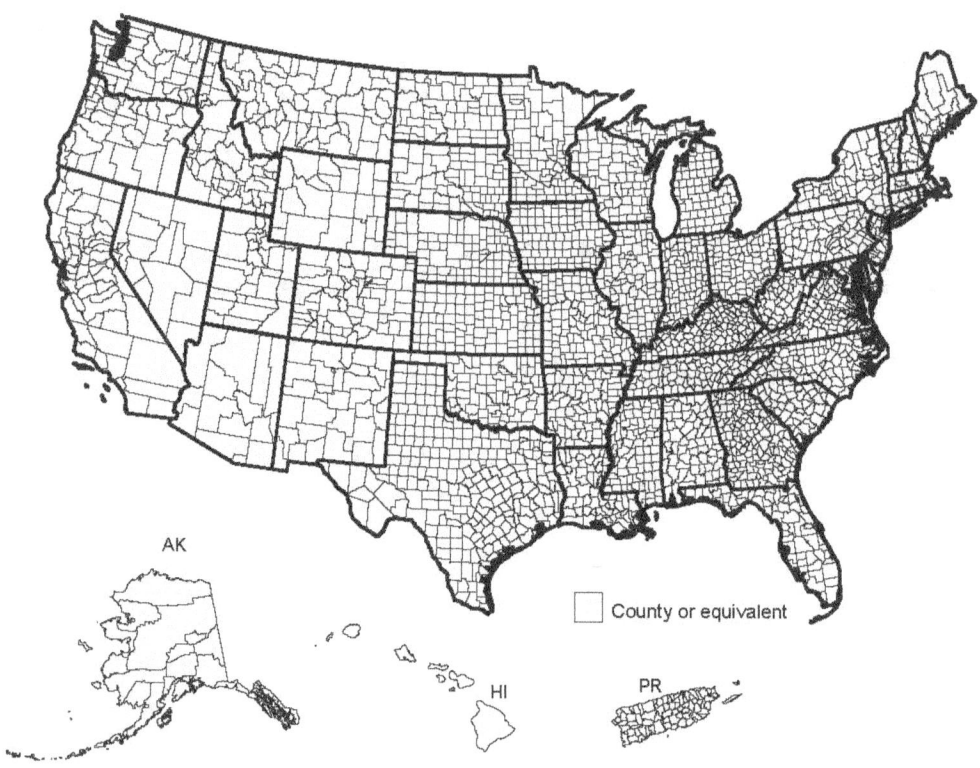

Figure 3—State and county (or equivalent) boundaries of the United States.

METHODS

Land Cover Map

The 2001 NLCD land cover map (Homer and others 2004, 2007) covers the 50 States, the District of Columbia, and Puerto Rico (hereafter, all are referred to as States). It has a spatial resolution of 0.09 ha (0.22 acres) per pixel. The original NLCD map legend identifies 16 land cover types (table 1) with a minimum mapping unit of five pixels (0.45 ha; 1.11 acres). The analyses of the NLCD map included adjacent ocean water area, but the map extent was limited to the boundaries of detailed State maps (ESRI 2005) (fig. 1) when preparing data summaries. The accuracy assessment of the 2001 NLCD has been reported in detail elsewhere (Wickham and others 2010).

The NLCD map legend was generalized to an eight-class legend and a three-class legend (table 1) for analyses. The eight-class legend was used to distinguish forest, grassland, and shrubland from other types of land cover. The three-class legend was used to implement the landscape mosaic measurements. An example map near Fort Collins, CO, (fig. 4) illustrates the different versions of the map legend. In the eight-class legend (fig. 4A), the northwest part of Fort Collins is represented by the large developed region, and the map extends west through agricultural, grassland/shrubland, and forest regions as the topography (not shown) extends from relatively flat ground through foothills to mountains.

Figure 4B illustrates the three-class legend, which highlights the developed and agriculture land cover types in relation to natural, i.e., neither agriculture nor developed, land cover types. Maps that show only one of the eight generalized land cover types identify shrubland (fig. 4C), grassland (fig. 4D), or forest (fig. 4E).

The patterns of any land cover type are influenced by the absolute amount of that land cover type that is present (e.g., if a given area is completely grassland, then the grassland pattern cannot be fragmented and conversely, if it contains only a small amount of grassland, then that grassland is more likely to appear fragmented). The percent of total area covered by the eight generalized land cover types is summarized nationally and by RPA region in table 2. The majority of States contain at least 20 percent forest land cover, but fewer than 15 States contain more than 20 percent grassland or shrubland land cover, and three States (the District of Columbia, Delaware, and Maryland) contain no grassland and no shrubland land cover (fig. 5). Similarly, pattern metrics describing proximity to anthropogenic land cover types depend on the presence of agriculture or developed land cover types. For example, there cannot be any agriculture-grassland interface if there is no agriculture land cover. The national picture of large and distinct regions dominated by forest, grassland, shrubland, or agriculture (fig. 1) is mirrored by maps of the county-level percents of those land cover types (fig. 6).

Table 1—Definition of land-cover legends used for the pattern analyses

NLCD legend[a]	Eight-class legend	Three-class legend
Water	Water	Natural
Perennial ice/snow	Water	Natural
Developed, open space	Developed	Developed
Developed, low intensity	Developed	Developed
Developed, medium intensity	Developed	Developed
Developed, high intensity	Developed	Developed
Barren land (rock/sand/clay)	Barren	Natural
Deciduous forest	Forest	Natural
Evergreen forest	Forest	Natural
Mixed forest	Forest	Natural
Shrub/scrub	Shrubland	Natural
Grassland/herbaceous	Grassland	Natural
Pasture/hay	Agriculture	Agriculture
Cultivated crops	Agriculture	Agriculture
Woody wetlands	Forest	Natural
Emergent herbaceous wetlands	Wetland	Natural

[a] Homer and others 2007.

Table 2—Percent of total area of eight generalized land cover types, national and by Forest and Rangeland Renewable Resources Planning Act of 1974 (RPA) region

RPA region	Water	Developed	Barren	Forest	Shrubland	Grassland	Agriculture	Wetland
	———————————————————————————Percent———————————————————————————							
Alaska	8.9	0.1	8.4	29.0	43.1	7.3	< 0.1	3.3
North	2.6	8.9	0.2	42.6	1.2	2.0	40.9	1.6
Pacific Coast	1.3	5.2	3.3	32.3	37.3	9.1	10.8	0.6
Rocky Mountain	1.1	2.1	1.9	16.3	33.9	27.3	16.8	0.7
South	2.2	7.1	0.4	39.2	15.2	11.0	23.2	1.8
National	2.9	4.5	2.4	30.1	25.2	13.8	19.5	1.6

Rows may not add up to 100 due to rounding off the figures.

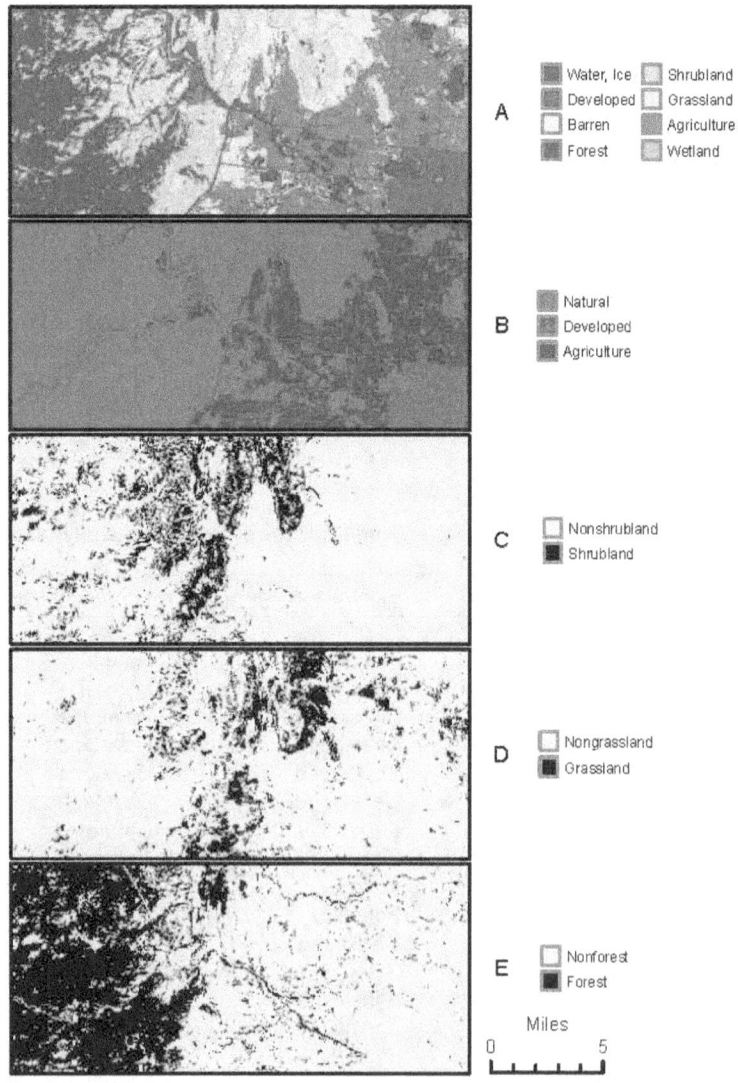

Figure 4—Preparation of input maps for pattern measurements; see text for explanation. Fort Collins, CO at lower right.

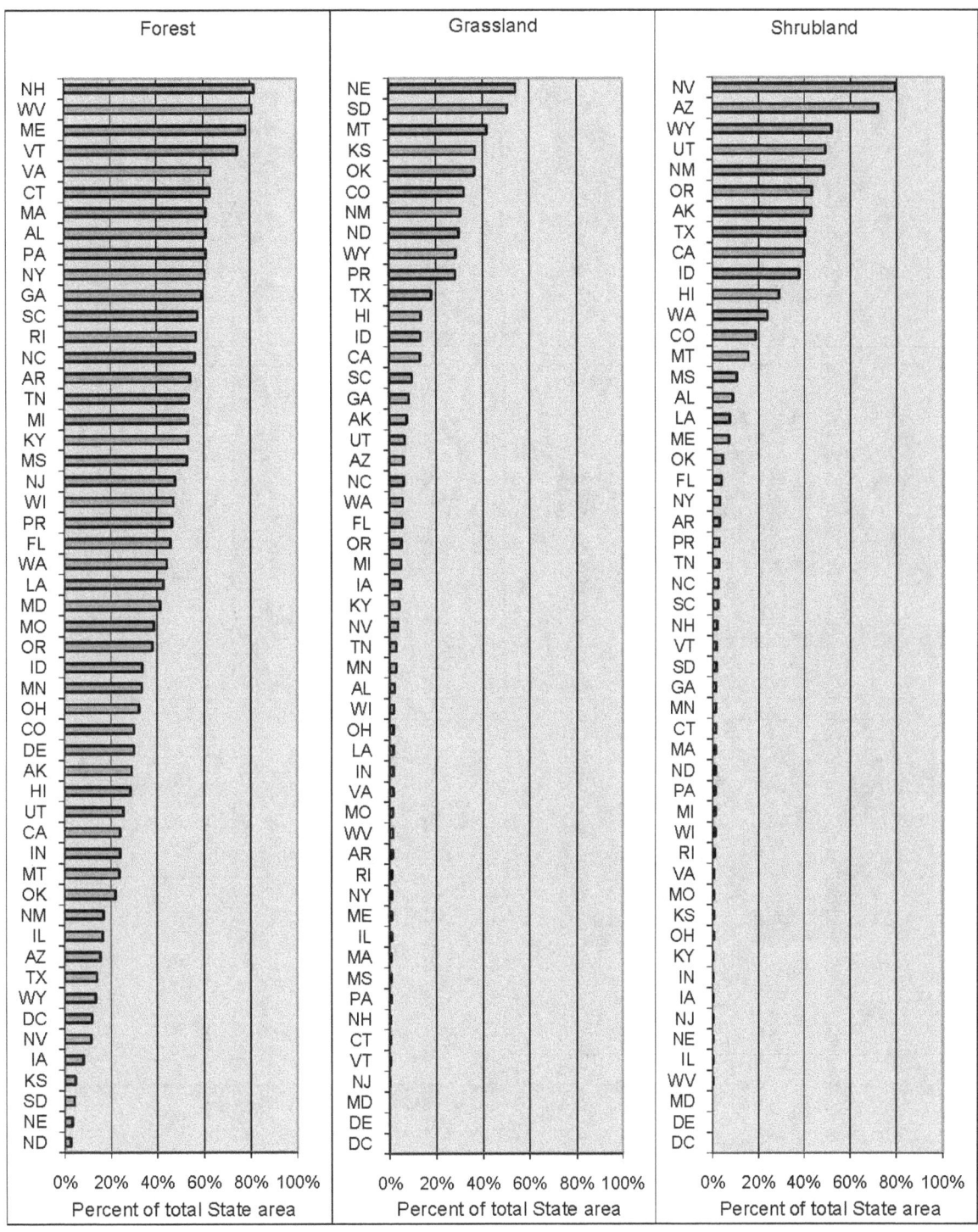

Figure 5—Percent of forest, grassland, and shrubland within each State. States are sorted in descending order separately for each land cover type.

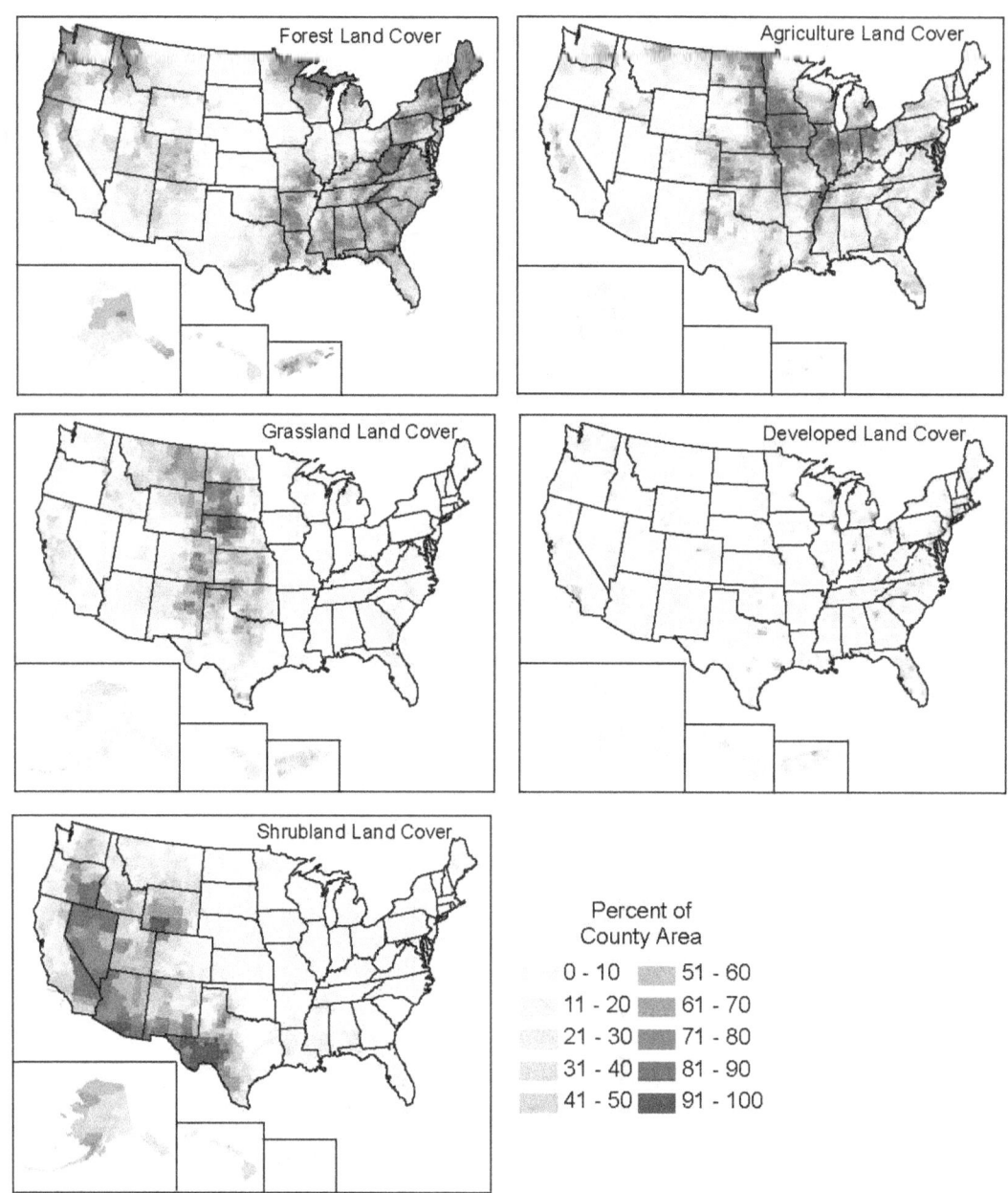

Figure 6—Percent of total county area with forest, grassland, shrubland, agriculture, and developed land cover.

Land Cover Patterns

Three basic pattern metrics—area density, landscape mosaic, and land cover structure—were measured on the NLCD land cover map. This section describes how the metrics were calculated, mapped, and summarized.

Area density—Area density is the proportion of a fixed-area neighborhood surrounding a location which is a given land cover type. Area density was measured separately for the forest (forest area density), grassland (grassland area density), and shrubland (shrubland area density) land cover types. At each location, the measurements were made within six neighborhood sizes which define six measurement scales[2]—10.9 acres, 37.6 acres, 162 acres, 1,460 acres, 13,100 acres, and 118,000 acres (fig. 7). Area density was measured as a proportion and was converted to an ordered categorical variable as one of seven area density classes: intact, interior, dominant, transitional, patchy, rare, and none (table 3). Along the gradient from intact to none, there is less of the given land cover type within the given neighborhood size. The classification of a given location may change with neighborhood size as more or less of the surrounding area is considered.

The area density measurements were implemented with a moving (overlapping) neighborhood algorithm that created new maps of the area density classes. For a given neighborhood size, the process began by centering the neighborhood on a subject pixel of the land cover map, measuring area density in that neighborhood, and determining the area density class (table 3), which was stored in a new map at the location of the subject pixel. The neighborhood was then centered on the adjacent subject pixel for the next measurement. In other words, for each neighborhood size and land cover type, the area density surrounding each pixel is calculated and stored in a new map. After repeating that process for all subject pixels on the land cover map, the result was a national map of area density classes with the same pixel size as the land cover map. A pixel value on such a map represents the area density class in the neighborhood of that pixel, i.e., it is a measure of the context of that pixel, not the contents of that pixel. The entire procedure was repeated separately

for forest, grassland, and shrubland, for each of the six neighborhood sizes, yielding a total of 18 national maps.

The mapped area density classes may be post-stratified or aggregated in different ways to answer different assessment questions. In this report, geographic stratifications were performed by aggregating pixel values nationally, within RPA regions, within States, and within counties. A landscape level summary includes all pixels within a geographic region, irrespective of the underlying land cover of those pixels. In some cases, a sector level summary was also prepared by selecting subsets of pixels according to their land cover type, i.e., their sector—forest, grassland, or shrubland. For example, forest area density values were summarized for all pixels in a State (landscape level) and for only the forest pixels in that State (sector level). The same measurement at a given location is used in both landscape level and sector level summaries, with the only difference whether a given location is included in a summary.

Figure 8 illustrates the area density measurements with a forest example. The input map (top left) was prepared by reclassifying the NLCD land cover as forest and nonforest land cover types. For this example, the moving neighborhood algorithm was applied with neighborhood sizes of 37.6 acres and 1,460 acres, yielding two landscape level maps (middle row), one for each neighborhood size. Two sector level maps (bottom row) were obtained by overlaying the forest map on the landscape level maps, retaining only the forest pixels. Note that the forest area density class "none" does not appear on the sector level map because every included pixel is a member of its own sector. For that reason, summaries of landscape level and sector level maps show seven and six area density classes, respectively. The examples in figure 8 also illustrate that the choice of neighborhood size serves to highlight either lower-frequency variance (larger neighborhood) or higher-frequency variance (smaller neighborhood) of forest area density; smaller neighborhood sizes are more robust to finer-scale forest patterns and larger neighborhoods are more robust to coarser-scale forest patterns.

Landscape mosaic—Landscape mosaic is the classification of a location according to the relative proportions of agriculture, developed, and natural (i.e., all other) land cover types in a neighborhood surrounding that location (Riitters and others 2000, 2009a). The natural land cover type includes forest, grassland, shrubland, water, barren, and wetland land cover types (table 1) because the landscape mosaic classification model is designed to highlight the juxtaposition of anthropogenic (agriculture or developed) land cover in

---

[2] Hereafter, neighborhood sizes are shown in acres with three significant digits. The exact neighborhood sizes in pixel dimensions and metric area units are: 7 pixels x 7 pixels or 4.410 ha (10.9 acres); 13 pixels x 13 pixels or 15.210 ha (37.6 acres); 27 pixels x 27 pixels or 65.610 ha (162 acres); 81 pixels x 81 pixels or 590.490 ha (1,460 acres); 243 pixels x 243 pixels or 5314.410 ha (13,100 acres); and; 729 pixels x 729 pixels or 47829.690 ha (118,000 acres).

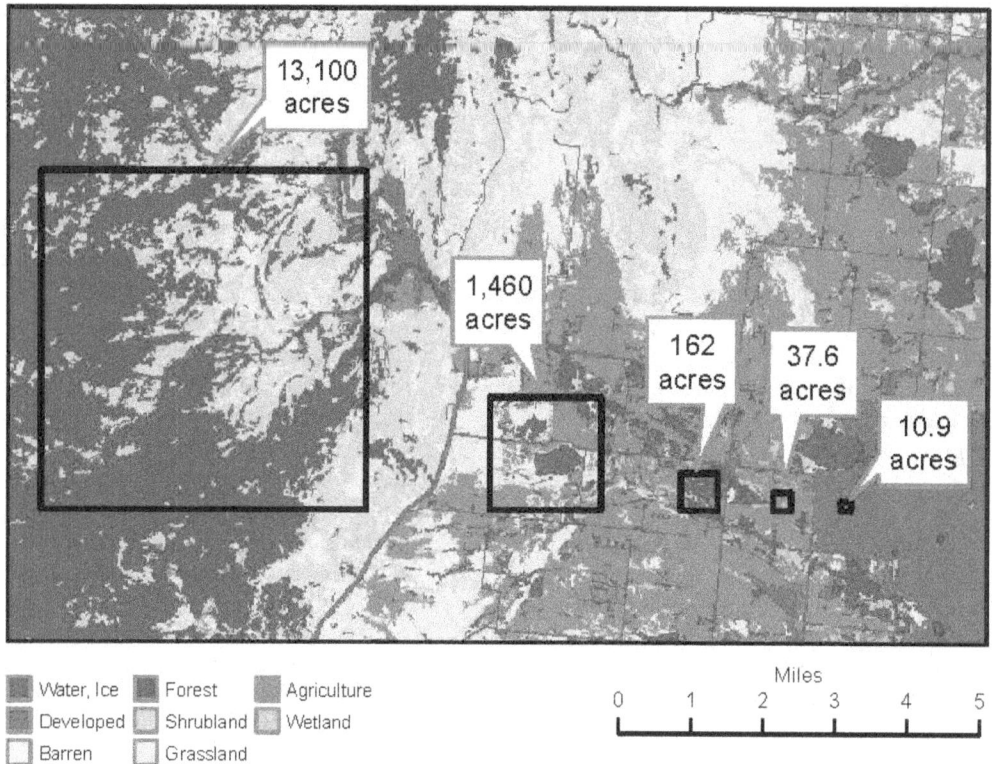

Figure 7—Relative sizes for five of the six neighborhoods used to measure the area density and landscape mosaic metrics. The largest neighborhood size (118,000 acres) is nine times greater than the largest neighborhood shown. Fort Collins, CO, at lower right.

Table 3—Area density class definitions

Area density class	Area density (p)
Intact	p = 1.0
Interior	0.9 ≤ p < 1.0
Dominant	0.6 ≤ p < 0.9
Transitional	0.4 ≤ p < 0.6
Patchy	0.1 ≤ p < 0.4
Rare	0.0 ≤ p < 0.1
None	p = 0.0

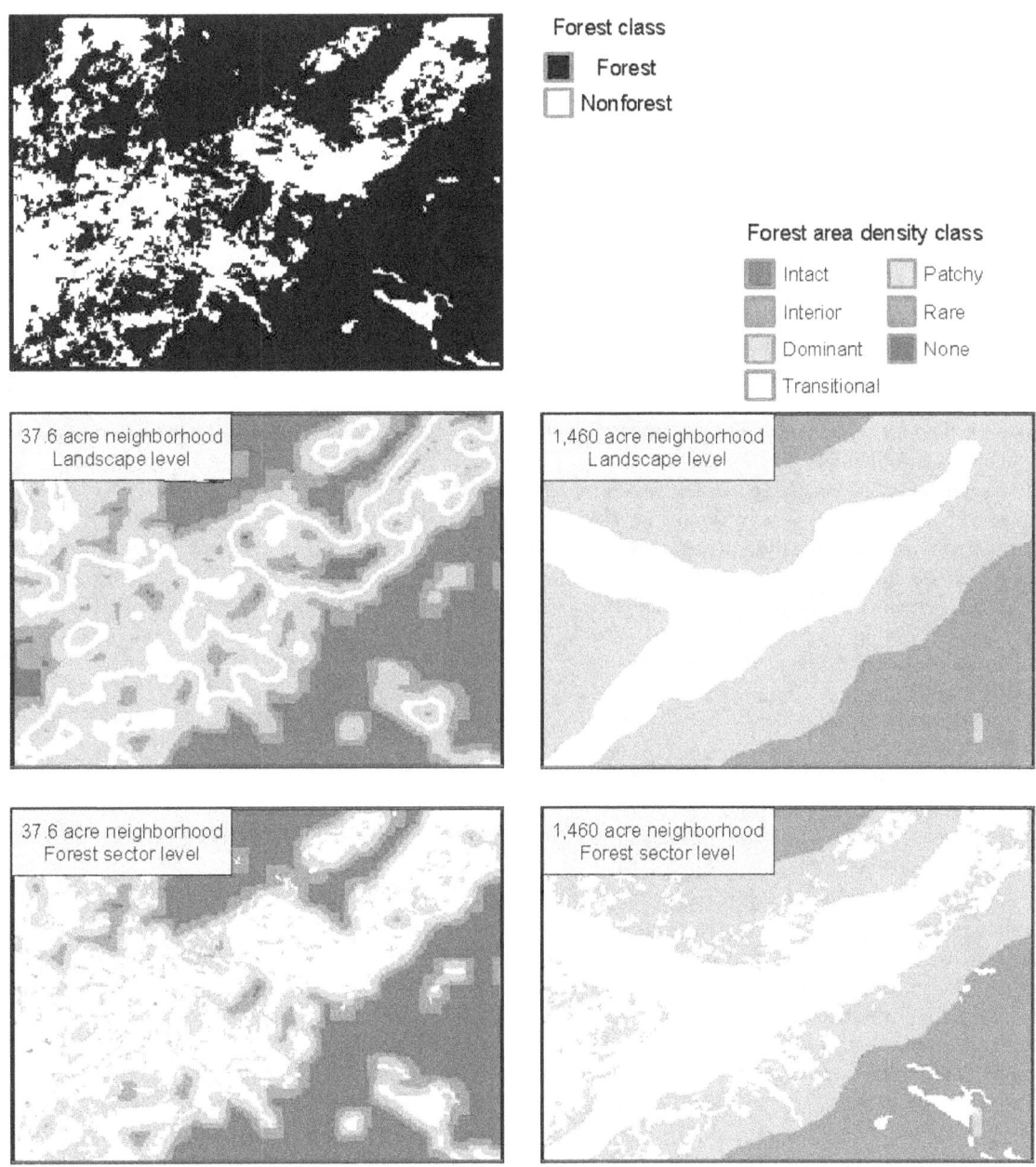

Figure 8—Forest area density classifications using two neighborhood sizes at landscape and sector levels; see text for explanation.

relation to natural land cover. The landscape mosaic model extends the well-known concept of the wildland-urban interface (Radeloff and others 2005, Stewart and others 2007) to other types of interfaces, using only a national land cover map as input data (Riitters and others 2000).

Like the area density measurements, the landscape mosaic was measured with a moving neighborhood algorithm using the same neighborhood sizes to produce six national maps of the landscape mosaic metric (one for each neighborhood size). To classify landscape mosaic from the NLCD land cover map, the land cover legend was condensed to the three-class legend (table 1). The proportions of agriculture, developed, and natural land cover types were then measured in the neighborhood of a given pixel, and a tri-polar classification model[3] (fig. 9) was used to assign one of 19 landscape mosaic classes to that neighborhood. The assigned value was stored at the location of the given pixel, and a national map of landscape mosaic was obtained after repeating the process for all pixels on the NLCD land cover map.

The nomenclature of the landscape mosaic legend is as follows: the letters D, A, and N refer to developed, agriculture, and natural, respectively. A letter appears in upper case if a neighborhood contains at least 60 percent of the corresponding land cover type, and in lower case if a neighborhood contains at least 10 percent but < 60 percent of that land cover type. A letter is absent if there is < 10 percent of that land cover type. Double upper case letters indicate neighborhoods that contain 100 percent of one land cover type. For example, a neighborhood classified as Ad contains at least 60 percent but < 100 percent agriculture, and at least 10 percent but < 60 percent developed land cover. The inset in figure 9 shows the colors used to create maps of the landscape mosaic metric; the intensities of the red, green, and blue components of a color are related to the proportions of the developed (red), natural (green), and agricultural (blue) land cover types.

Landscape level summaries of landscape mosaic include every pixel in a geographic region, while sector level summaries include only pixels of a given land cover type. Both types of summaries were prepared nationally, by RPA region, by State, and by county. Figure 10 illustrates landscape mosaic mapping with a forest sector example.

---

[3] The model is analogous to the 'soil triangle' classification model (Gee and Bauder 1986) by which soil texture is classified according to the fractions of sand, silt, and clay in a soil sample. Here, the measured proportions of agriculture, developed, and natural land cover in a neighborhood replace the proportions of sand, silt, and clay in a soil sample.

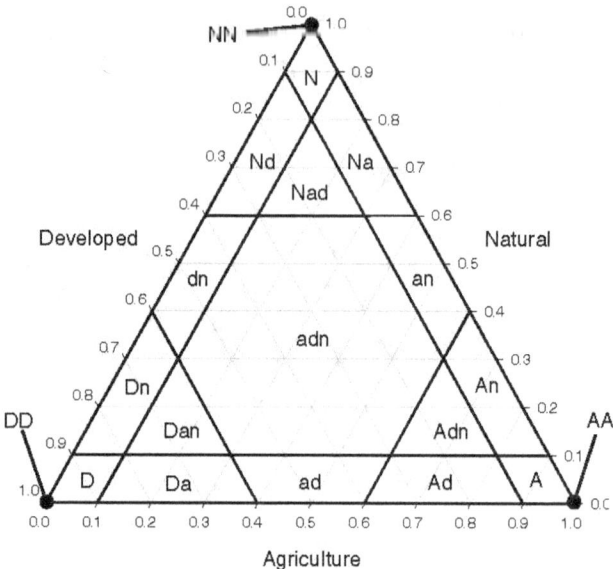

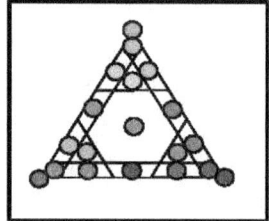

Figure 9—Landscape mosaic classification model; see text for explanation. Inset shows colors used to render maps of landscape mosaics.

The input map (top) was prepared by converting the NLCD land cover map to a map of natural, developed, and agriculture land cover types (table 1). For this example, the moving neighborhood algorithm was applied with neighborhood sizes of 37.6 acres and 1,460 acres, yielding two landscape level maps (middle row). Two sector level maps (bottom row) were obtained by overlaying the forest-nonforest map (not shown; a subset of the natural pixels) on the landscape level maps, retaining only the forest pixels. Comparable sector level maps for grassland and shrubland would be obtained by overlaying maps of grassland and shrubland on the same landscape level maps, retaining only the grassland or shrubland pixels. The landscape mosaic classes DD and AA do not appear on a forest, grassland, or shrubland sector level map because every included location has at least one natural pixel (i.e., the location itself) in its neighborhood. Smaller neighborhood sizes are more robust to finer-scale patterns, and larger neighborhoods are more robust to coarser-scale patterns.

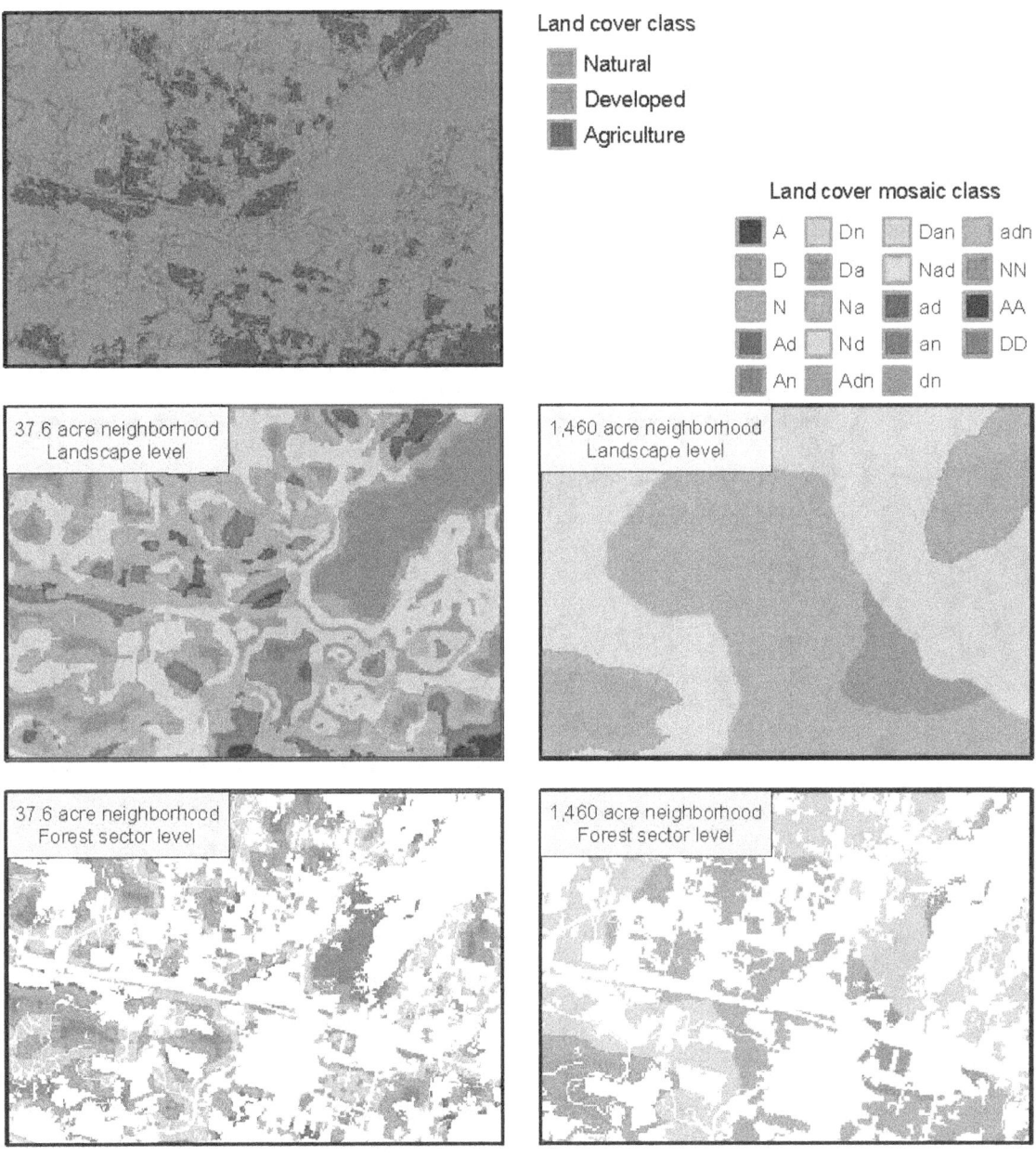

Figure 10—Landscape mosaic classifications using two neighborhood sizes at landscape and sector levels; see text for explanation.

The 19 landscape mosaic classes were combined in different ways to highlight several uses of the landscape mosaic information (fig. 11). Landscape mosaic was converted to landscape background by grouping the 19 classes into four classes that indicate if the neighborhood is dominated by (i.e., contains at least 60 percent of) developed, agriculture, or natural land cover, or is not dominated by any of them (fig. 11, top). Landscape background is indicative of the types of anthropogenic influences (e.g., edge effects versus matrix effects) likely to operate in a given landscape (Riitters and others 2009b). Landscape mosaic was also converted to two versions of landscape interface by different groupings of the 19 landscape mosaic classes. Three types of developed interface (fig. 11, middle) identify locations dominated by developed land cover (developed-dominant), or containing

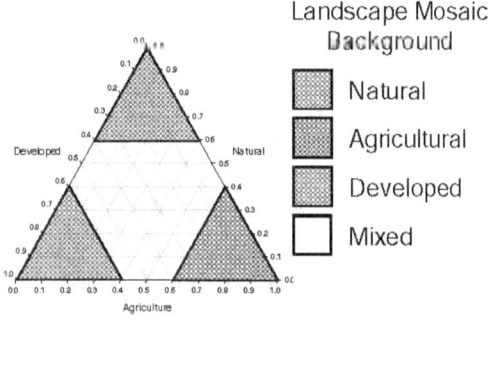

Landscape Mosaic
Background

- ▨ Natural
- ▨ Agricultural
- ▨ Developed
- ☐ Mixed

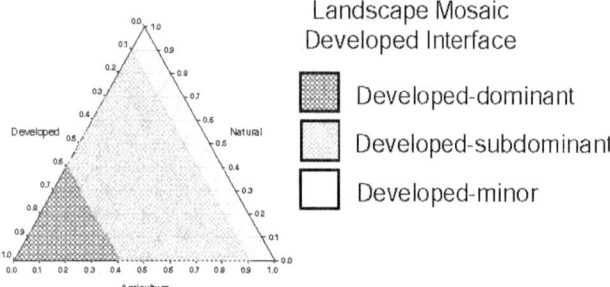

Landscape Mosaic
Developed Interface

- ▨ Developed-dominant
- ▨ Developed-subdominant
- ☐ Developed-minor

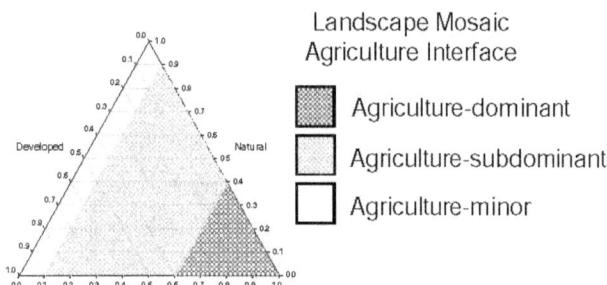

Landscape Mosaic
Agriculture Interface

- ▨ Agriculture-dominant
- ▨ Agriculture-subdominant
- ☐ Agriculture-minor

Figure 11—Simplifications of the landscape mosaic classification model used to identify four landscape background classes (top), three developed interface classes (center), and three agriculture interface classes (bottom); see text for explanation.

at least 10 percent but < 60 percent developed land cover (developed-subdominant), or containing < 10 percent developed land cover (developed-minor). Three types of agriculture interface (fig. 11, bottom) called agriculture-dominant, agriculture-subdominant, and agriculture-minor are analogous to developed interface. In the case of landscape interfaces, different neighborhood sizes are conceptually similar to different buffer distances (Stewart and others 2007).

Land cover structure—The land cover structure of a given location refers to the structural role that is played by that location in relation to nearby locations of the same land cover type. Land cover structure was measured separately for forest, grassland, and shrubland using the morphological spatial pattern analysis algorithm described by Soille and Vogt (2009) (see also Vogt and others 2007a, 2007b).[4] The algorithm assigns each pixel of forest, grassland, or shrubland to one of 11 mutually exclusive structure classes (table 4), depending on the scale parameter of edge width (Soille and Vogt 2009). For each land cover type, the algorithm begins by identifying core structures as the subset of pixels of that land cover type that are more than the edge width distance away from a different land cover type. The remaining pixels are subdivided according to their location and connectedness with respect to core. The perforated pixels form interior perimeters (within core) and the edge pixels form exterior perimeters (around core). The connector pixels link different clusters of core and the islet pixels are not linked to core.

For this report, the measurements were made with four edge widths[5] which define four measurement scales: 98 feet, 197 feet, 394 feet, and 787 feet. The structural role played by a given pixel may change with edge width (Ostapowicz and others 2008, Vogt and others 2007a) (e.g., a pixel may be core when edges are relatively narrow, but that same pixel may be part of a connector when edges are relatively wider). For this report, the 11 structure classes were combined into six classes (table 4): core, perforated, edge, connector, branch, and islet. These classes are useful in identifying structural phase transitions in dynamic landscapes (Riitters and others 2007).

Figure 12 illustrates land cover structure classification with a forest sector example. The input map (fig. 12, top) was prepared by converting the NLCD land cover map to a forest–nonforest map (table 1). In this example, the classification was performed with edge widths of 98 feet (fig. 12, middle) and 787 feet (fig. 12, bottom). The examples show that increasing the edge width parameter reduces the amount of the core class, and may change the classification of the remaining forest pixels. A smaller edge width parameter is more robust to finer-scale patterns while larger parameter values are more robust to coarser-scale patterns. Unlike the area density and landscape mosaic

---

[4] See also the URL http://forest.jrc.ec.europa.eu/download/software/guidos for additional examples and documentation of the GUIDOS software.
[5] Hereafter the edge widths are rounded to the nearest foot. The exact edge widths (m) are: 30 m (98 feet); 60 m (197 feet); 120 m (394 feet), and 240 m (787 feet).

metrics, the land cover structure metric is by definition a sector level metric because it only addresses a single land cover type. Sector level summaries were prepared nationally, by RPA region, by State, and by county.

Implementation summary—Table 5 summarizes the implementation of metrics for this report. Thirty-six national maps of land cover patterns were produced from the 2001 NLCD land cover map, including: forest, grassland, and shrubland area density maps at six measurement scales (18 maps), landscape mosaic at six measurement scales (6 maps), and forest, grassland, and shrubland structure maps at four measurement scales each (12 maps). The 36 derived maps are geographically comparable on a pixel by pixel basis with the NLCD map and with each other. The area density maps were summarized at landscape level (seven area density classes) by including every pixel in a defined geographic region, and at three sector levels (forest, grassland, and shrubland; six area density classes) by including only the pixels of a given land cover type. The landscape mosaic maps were summarized at landscape level (four landscape background classes) and at three sector levels (forest, grassland, shrubland; four landscape background classes, three developed interface classes, and

three agriculture interface classes). The land cover structure maps were produced and summarized at the sector level for the forest, grassland, and shrubland sectors.

Notes on States and Counties

The 52 States referred to in this report include the 50 actual States along with the District of Columbia and Puerto Rico. Since Delaware, the District of Columbia, and Maryland contained no grassland and no shrubland, the State sector level statistics for grassland and shrubland land cover patterns are missing for those States. This report recognized a total of 3,219 geographic units referred to as counties (fig. 3), including 3,007 true counties, 16 boroughs and 11 census areas (in Arkansas), 64 parishes (in Louisiana), 78 Municipios (in Puerto Rico), a district (the District of Columbia), and 42 independent cities (one each in Maryland, Missouri, and Nevada, and 39 in Virginia). Four counties contained no forest land cover, 212 counties contained no grassland land cover, and 395 counties contained no shrubland land cover. In the sector level county maps shown in this report, the counties lacking a given cover-type are shown as missing counties.

Table 4—Conversion of MSPA (morphological spatial pattern analysis) classes to structure classes

MSPA class[a]	Structure class	Description[b]
Core	Core	Foreground pixels whose distance to the background is greater than the edge width
Islet	Islet	Cluster of foreground pixels that is too small to contain core, and is not a connector or branch

Perforation
  Bridge in perforation
  Loop in perforation
	Perforated	The interior perimeter around a hole (inclusion) in a cluster of core pixels

Edge
  Bridge in edge
  Loop in edge
	Edge	The exterior perimeter around a cluster of core pixels

Bridge Loop	Connector	Cluster of pixels linking two or more edge pixels, or two or more perforated pixels
Branch	Branch	Cluster of pixels connected to one edge pixel or one perforated pixel

[a] Soille and Vogt (2009).
[b] "Foreground" is the one analyzed land cover type (forest, grassland, or shrubland) and "background" is the complement of foreground; "edge width" is an analysis parameter.

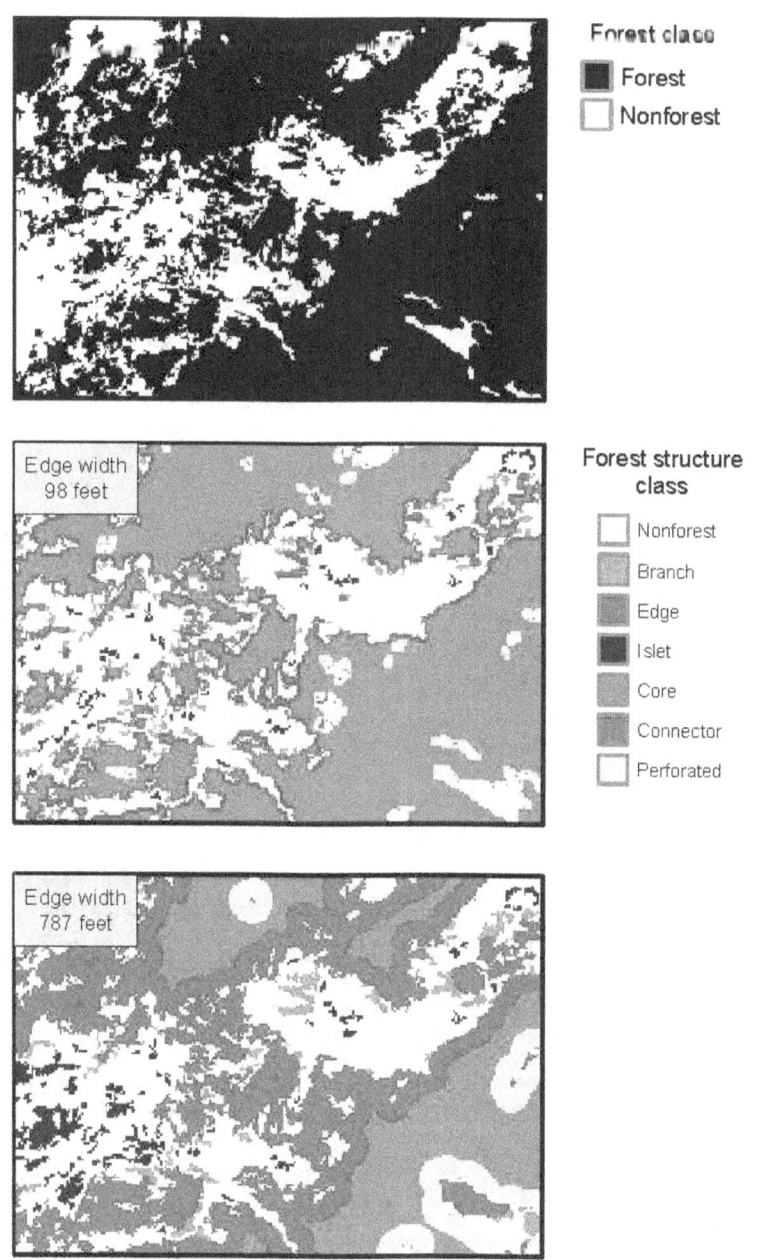

Figure 12—Forest structure classifications using two edge widths at sector level; see text for explanation.

Table 5—Land cover pattern metrics and measurement scales summarized at landscape and sector levels

Metric	Measurement scale units	Landscape level	Sector level
Area density	Neighborhood size	Forest area density Grassland area density Shrubland area density	Forest area density Grassland area density Shrubland area density
Landscape mosaic	Neighborhood size	Landscape background	Forest background Grassland background Shrubland background Forest-agriculture interface Forest-developed interface Grassland-agriculture interface Grassland-developed interface Shrubland-agriculture interface Shrubland-developed interface
Land cover structure	Edge width		Forest structure Grassland structure Shrubland structure

RESULTS

Landscape Level Statistics

The landscape level statistics for the area density and landscape background metrics describe land cover patterns in terms of the total area within geographic strata. National and regional results are presented in tabular form for all six neighborhood sizes (measurement scales). Representative statistics are illustrated by State in stacked bar charts for the 37.6-acre and 1,460-acre neighborhood sizes, and by county in maps for the 1,460-acre neighborhood size.

Area density—The national and regional percent of total area in seven area density classes is shown for six neighborhood sizes in table 6 (forest), table 7 (grassland), and table 8 (shrubland). The comparable State results for 37.6-acre and 1,460-acre neighborhood sizes are illustrated in figure 13 (forest), figure 14 (grassland), and figure 15 (shrubland). The percent of total area that is either intact or interior area density may help in identifying regions containing large tracts of relatively unfragmented land cover; figure 16 illustrates the percent of total county area characterized as either intact or interior for forest, grassland, and shrubland for a neighborhood size of 1,460 acres.

Landscape background—Table 9 shows the national and regional percent of total area in four landscape background classes for six neighborhood sizes. The comparable State statistics are shown in figure 17 for neighborhood sizes of 37.6 acres and 1,460 acres. Figure 18 illustrates the comparable percent of total county area in four landscape background classes for a neighborhood size of 1,460 acres.

Sector Level Statistics

The sector level statistics for the area density, landscape mosaic, and structure metrics describe forest, grassland, or shrubland as a fraction of the total area of each land cover type within geographic strata. National and regional results are presented in tabular form for six neighborhood sizes for the area density and landscape mosaic metrics, and four edge widths for the structure metrics. Comparable results by State are illustrated in stacked bar charts for two neighborhood sizes (37.6 acres and 1,460 acres) or two edge widths (98 feet and 787 feet). Selected aspects of pattern metrics are illustrated by county in maps for a neighborhood size of 1,460 acres or an edge width of 787 feet.

Area density—The national and regional percent of total forest area in six forest area density classes (table 10), grassland area in six grassland area density classes (table

11), and shrubland area in six shrubland area density classes (table 12) is shown for six neighborhood sizes. Comparable statistics for neighborhood sizes of 37.6 acres and 1,460 acres are shown by State for forest (fig. 19), grassland (fig. 20), and shrubland (fig. 21). The percent of forest, grassland, or shrubland area that is either intact or interior area density may help in identifying regions where the current land cover is relatively unfragmented, considering the amount of a land cover that is present. Figure 22 illustrates the percent of total forest, grassland, or shrubland area within a county that is either intact or interior forest, grassland, and shrubland for a neighborhood size of 1,460 acres (compare to figure 16).

Landscape background—Tables 13, 14, and 15 show the national and regional percent of total forest, grassland, and shrubland area, respectively, in four landscape background classes for six neighborhood sizes. Comparable State statistics are shown for neighborhood sizes of 37.6 acres and 1,460 acres in figure 23 (forest), figure 24 (grassland), and figure 25 (shrubland). The percent of a given land cover type that is in the mixed background class may help in identifying regions with high proportions of current forest, grassland, and shrubland in landscapes undergoing transitions from natural to anthropogenic dominance; figure 26 illustrates the county percent of total forest, grassland, and shrubland area that is in the mixed landscape background class for a neighborhood size of 1,460 acres.

Landscape interfaces—Tables 16, 17, and 18 contain the national and regional percent of total forest, grassland, and shrubland area, respectively, in three developed interface classes and three agriculture interface classes, for six neighborhood sizes. Note that a given location is in both a developed interface and an agriculture interface; the row totals are 100 percent within each type of interface.

The State percent of forest (fig. 27), grassland (fig. 28), and shrubland (fig. 29) in three developed interface classes is shown for neighborhood sizes of 37.6 acres and 1,460 acres. The percent of those land cover types in either the developed-dominant or developed-subdominant classes may help to identify counties with high fractions of the existing forest, grassland, and shrubland in a developed interface zone; figure 30 illustrates those county percents for a neighborhood size of 1,460 acres.

The State percent of forest (fig. 31), grassland (fig. 32), and shrubland (fig. 33) in three agriculture interface classes is shown for neighborhood sizes of 37.6 acres and 1,460 acres. The percent of those land cover types in either the agriculture-dominant or agriculture-subdominant classes may help in identifying counties with high fractions of the existing forest, grassland, and shrubland in an agriculture interface zone; figure 34 illustrates those county percents for a neighborhood size of 1,460 acres.

Land cover structure—The national and regional percent of total forest, grassland, and shrubland area in six structure classes for four edge widths is shown in tables 19, 20, and 21, respectively. Comparable State statistics for edge widths of 98 feet and 787 feet are shown for forest (fig. 35), grassland (fig. 36), and shrubland (fig. 37). The percent of

a given land cover type that is in the connector class may help in identifying regions where management of existing movement pathways (corridors) is likely of concern, while islet class percent may help in identifying regions where management could be aimed at the formation of such pathways between isolated fragments of land cover. Figures 38 and 39 illustrate the percent of total forest, grassland, and shrubland area within a county in the connector class and islet class, respectively, for a 787-foot edge width.

Table 6—Forest area density, landscape level. Percent of total area in seven forest area density classes, for six neighborhood sizes, by Forest and Rangeland Renewable Resources Planning Act of 1974 (RPA) region and national

Neighborhood size	Region	None	Rare	Patchy	Transitional	Dominant	Interior	Intact
					-----Percent-----			
10.9 acres	Alaska	55.0	4.0	9.7	5.0	8.1	4.2	14.0
	North	35.3	5.3	13.1	7.1	12.7	6.1	20.5
	Pacific Coast	53.3	3.1	8.2	5.0	9.9	5.0	15.4
	Rocky Mountain	73.0	3.1	6.6	2.9	4.5	2.2	7.7
	South	38.3	5.1	13.6	7.7	12.8	5.9	16.7
	National	53.1	4.1	10.1	5.4	9.0	4.4	13.9
37.6 acres	Alaska	48.7	8.6	11.0	5.7	10.3	6.8	8.9
	North	25.6	10.8	16.7	8.8	16.2	10.1	11.9
	Pacific Coast	48.4	6.0	9.4	5.9	12.9	8.5	8.8
	Rocky Mountain	67.1	7.7	7.8	3.3	5.6	3.6	4.8
	South	30.0	9.1	16.9	9.8	16.5	9.0	8.7
	National	46.0	8.6	12.3	6.5	11.6	7.1	8.1
162 acres	Alaska	41.1	14.0	12.6	6.7	12.6	9.2	3.7
	North	15.1	16.1	20.8	10.9	19.8	13.1	4.1
	Pacific Coast	42.9	9.4	10.5	6.9	16.4	10.9	2.9
	Rocky Mountain	58.3	15.3	9.0	3.8	6.9	5.0	1.9
	South	22.4	11.9	19.8	12.8	20.7	9.8	2.6
	National	37.6	13.9	14.5	8.0	14.3	8.9	2.8
1,460 acres	Alaska	33.4	18.5	15.0	8.6	15.6	8.7	0.3
	North	7.0	18.7	25.5	13.2	24.2	11.3	0.2
	Pacific Coast	36.6	13.0	11.9	8.2	21.1	9.0	0.1
	Rocky Mountain	47.0	24.8	10.5	4.4	8.4	4.7	0.1
	South	16.0	13.7	21.7	16.9	25.8	5.8	0.2
	National	29.1	18.9	16.8	10.0	17.8	7.2	0.2
13,100 acres	Alaska	27.1	21.3	18.1	10.4	17.6	5.4	0.0
	North	3.2	18.7	28.9	14.1	27.7	7.3	0.0
	Pacific Coast	30.4	16.5	13.8	9.9	24.8	4.7	0.0
	Rocky Mountain	36.3	33.3	12.5	5.6	9.7	2.6	0.0
	South	12.4	14.4	22.6	20.1	28.0	2.5	0.0
	National	22.5	22.7	19.0	11.8	20.0	4.1	0.0
118,000 acres	Alaska	21.3	23.2	22.4	12.3	18.2	2.5	0.0
	North	0.8	18.5	31.8	14.7	30.5	3.9	0.0
	Pacific Coast	22.8	19.0	18.8	12.1	26.1	1.2	0.0
	Rocky Mountain	24.0	41.6	16.9	7.5	9.2	0.8	0.0
	South	9.6	14.8	23.4	23.4	28.0	0.8	0.0
	National	15.7	26.0	22.2	13.8	20.6	1.7	0.0

Rows may not add up to 100 due to rounding off the figures.

Table 7—Grassland area density, landscape level. Percent of total area in seven grassland area density classes, for six neighborhood sizes, by Forest and Rangeland Renewable Resources Planning Act of 1974 (RPA) region and national

Neighborhood size	Region	None	Rare	Patchy	Transitional	Dominant	Interior	Intact
					Percent			
10.9 acres	Alaska	82.2	3.3	6.9	2.5	2.6	0.9	1.6
	North	90.2	3.5	5.0	0.8	0.4	0.1	0.1
	Pacific Coast	78.1	4.2	8.2	2.9	3.3	1.1	2.2
	Rocky Mountain	54.1	5.0	11.7	5.4	7.9	3.2	12.7
	South	71.0	6.4	11.6	3.5	3.8	1.2	2.5
	National	71.5	4.7	9.4	3.4	4.3	1.6	5.2
37.6 acres	Alaska	76.7	8.2	7.8	2.6	2.9	1.0	0.7
	North	82.2	11.6	5.3	0.5	0.2	0.0	0.0
	Pacific Coast	70.0	11.2	9.9	3.1	3.5	1.3	1.1
	Rocky Mountain	45.4	11.4	14.0	6.2	9.2	5.5	8.3
	South	59.8	16.3	13.5	3.8	4.0	1.4	1.2
	National	62.9	12.1	10.9	3.7	4.8	2.4	3.2
162 acres	Alaska	69.2	14.6	9.1	2.9	3.1	0.9	0.2
	North	67.1	27.3	5.2	0.3	0.1	0.0	0.0
	Pacific Coast	57.5	22.0	12.1	3.2	3.4	1.4	0.4
	Rocky Mountain	34.7	18.9	17.1	7.5	10.7	7.3	3.9
	South	45.4	28.9	16.0	4.1	4.0	1.3	0.4
	National	50.8	22.4	12.9	4.2	5.3	3.0	1.4
1,460 acres	Alaska	62.2	20.5	10.6	3.2	3.0	0.5	0.0
	North	48.6	47.0	4.3	0.1	0.0	0.0	0.0
	Pacific Coast	42.2	35.7	14.7	3.3	3.1	1.0	0.0
	Rocky Mountain	24.6	24.2	21.5	9.4	12.6	7.1	0.6
	South	33.1	39.1	18.6	4.5	3.9	0.7	0.0
	National	38.7	32.4	15.3	5.0	5.8	2.7	0.2
13,100 acres	Alaska	56.6	25.2	11.9	3.4	2.7	0.3	0.0
	North	37.5	58.9	3.6	0.0	0.0	0.0	0.0
	Pacific Coast	30.0	46.4	17.0	3.4	2.7	0.5	0.0
	Rocky Mountain	17.5	27.2	25.6	11.1	13.6	5.0	0.0
	South	27.1	44.2	19.7	5.1	3.7	0.3	0.0
	National	30.9	38.5	17.1	5.7	6.0	1.8	0.0
118,000 acres	Alaska	50.5	30.8	13.1	3.3	2.2	0.1	0.0
	North	30.3	66.9	2.8	0.0	0.0	0.0	0.0
	Pacific Coast	19.7	54.8	20.2	3.6	1.8	0.0	0.0
	Rocky Mountain	10.7	30.0	29.5	13.0	13.9	3.0	0.0
	South	23.3	47.3	20.4	5.5	3.3	0.0	0.0
	National	24.6	43.3	18.9	6.4	5.8	1.0	0.0

Rows may not add up to 100 due to rounding off the figures.

Table 8—Shrubland area density, landscape level. Percent of total area in seven shrubland area density classes, for six neighborhood sizes, by Forest and Rangeland Renewable Resources Planning Act of 1974 (RPA) region and national

Neighborhood size	Region	None	Rare	Patchy	Transitional	Dominant	Interior	Intact
					-------Percent-------			
10.9 acres	Alaska	33.8	5.3	13.8	7.9	13.2	6.6	19.4
	North	93.5	2.6	3.2	0.4	0.2	0.0	0.0
	Pacific Coast	39.7	6.2	14.8	6.6	8.6	3.4	20.8
	Rocky Mountain	49.2	4.0	10.6	5.6	8.1	3.5	19.1
	South	68.7	5.7	10.1	3.3	4.0	1.5	6.7
	National	58.6	4.5	10.0	4.5	6.5	2.9	12.9
37.6 acres	Alaska	25.7	10.6	15.9	8.9	16.5	10.4	11.9
	North	88.0	8.6	3.0	0.3	0.1	0.0	0.0
	Pacific Coast	29.5	13.4	18.2	7.3	9.5	5.3	16.7
	Rocky Mountain	43.2	8.3	12.3	6.1	9.4	5.6	15.1
	South	59.0	14.6	11.4	3.3	4.3	2.3	5.0
	National	51.1	10.7	11.5	5.0	7.7	4.5	9.6
162 acres	Alaska	17.2	15.6	18.6	10.6	19.7	13.6	4.8
	North	77.3	19.8	2.7	0.2	0.1	0.0	0.0
	Pacific Coast	18.7	20.3	22.7	8.0	10.1	8.1	12.0
	Rocky Mountain	36.6	12.6	14.4	6.8	10.4	8.6	10.5
	South	46.0	26.0	13.5	3.4	4.4	3.3	3.3
	National	41.5	18.3	13.5	5.5	8.6	6.5	6.1
1,460 acres	Alaska	9.7	17.4	23.2	13.6	22.9	12.7	0.5
	North	67.0	30.6	2.3	0.1	0.0	0.0	0.0
	Pacific Coast	10.5	23.0	29.0	8.7	11.1	12.8	4.9
	Rocky Mountain	31.3	14.8	17.4	7.8	11.9	12.7	4.1
	South	36.3	33.6	16.2	3.4	4.6	4.7	1.2
	National	33.7	23.4	16.3	6.3	9.7	8.5	2.2
13,100 acres	Alaska	5.6	15.8	28.7	16.6	24.7	8.7	0.0
	North	61.7	36.3	1.9	0.0	0.0	0.0	0.0
	Pacific Coast	7.1	20.5	34.9	10.0	12.7	14.3	0.3
	Rocky Mountain	28.1	14.8	20.0	9.1	14.2	13.3	0.4
	South	30.6	37.7	17.8	3.6	4.9	5.2	0.1
	National	29.3	24.9	18.9	7.4	11.0	8.3	0.2
118,000 acres	Alaska	2.9	12.5	34.9	19.6	25.7	4.5	0.0
	North	57.9	40.4	1.6	0.0	0.0	0.0	0.0
	Pacific Coast	4.7	16.7	41.0	11.7	14.9	11.0	0.0
	Rocky Mountain	25.3	14.0	22.5	10.6	17.9	9.7	0.0
	South	26.0	41.1	18.8	4.0	5.3	4.8	0.0
	National	26.0	25.3	21.5	8.6	12.6	6.0	0.0

Rows may not add up to 100 due to rounding off the figures.

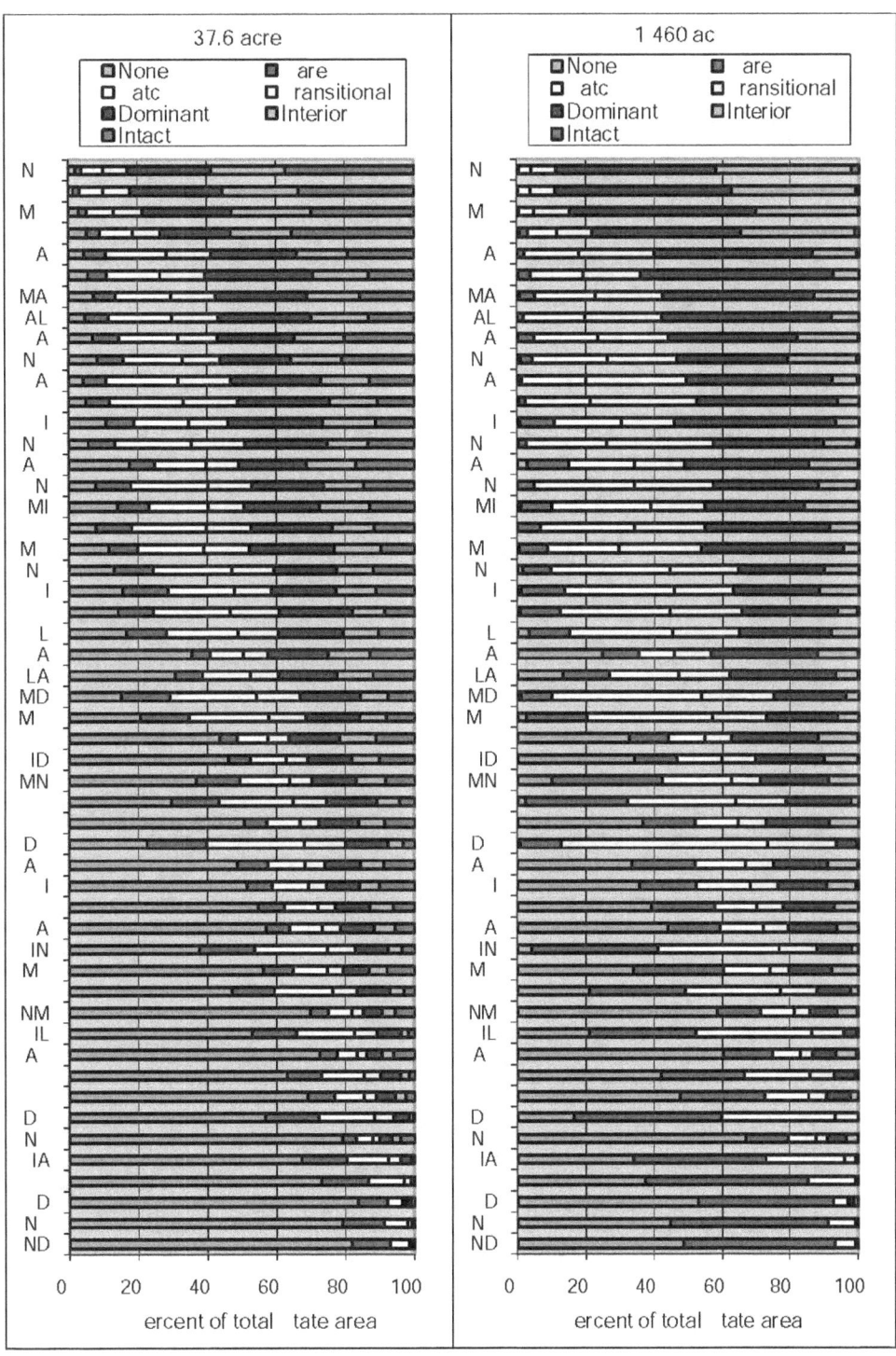

Figure 13—Percent of total State area in seven forest area density classes for neighborhood sizes of 37.6 acres (left) and 1,460 acres (right). States are sorted in descending order by percent forest (see fig. 5).

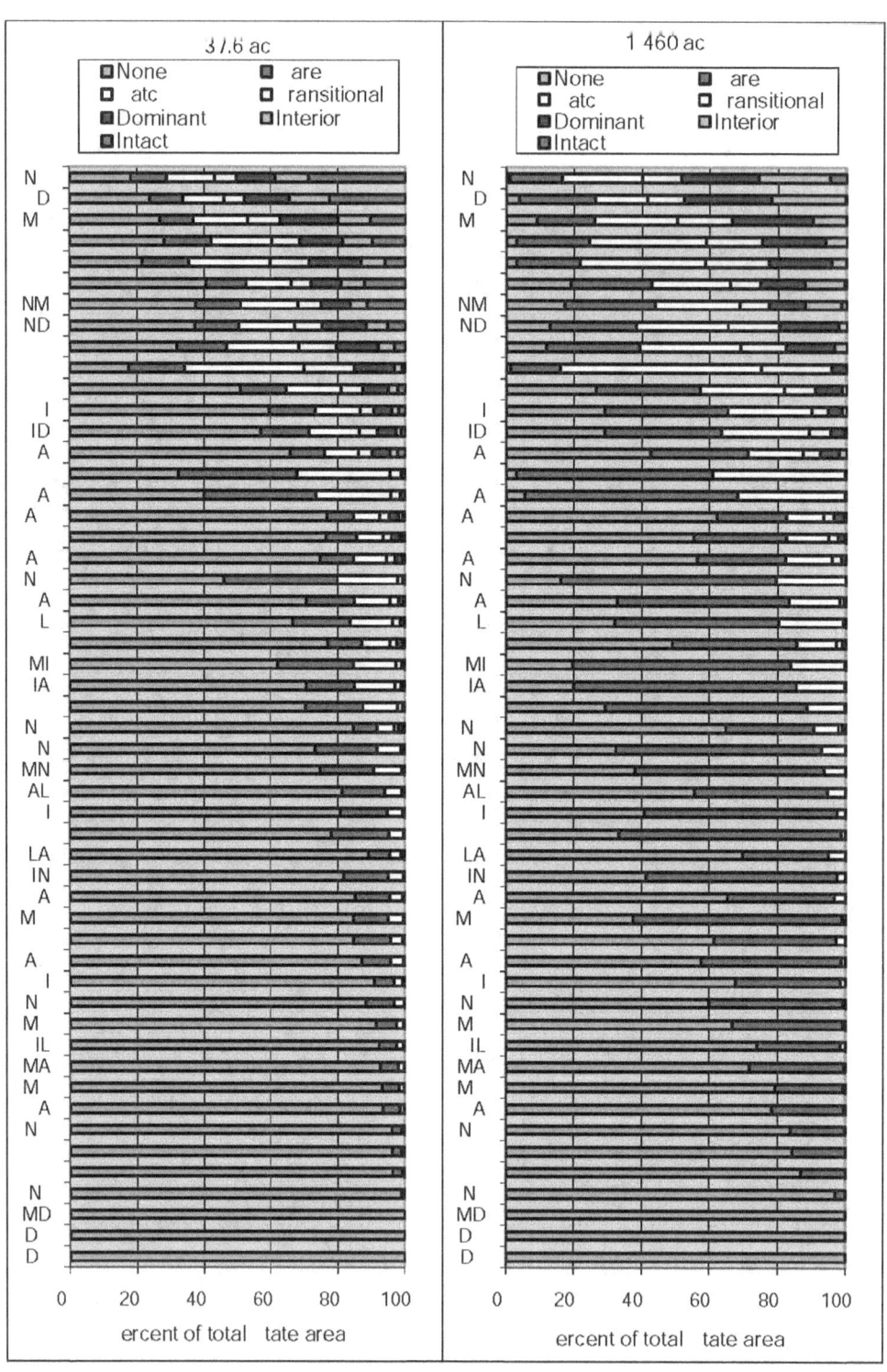

Figure 14—Percent of total State area in seven grassland area density classes for neighborhood sizes of 37.6 acres (left) and 1,460 acres (right). States are sorted in descending order by percent grassland (see fig. 5).

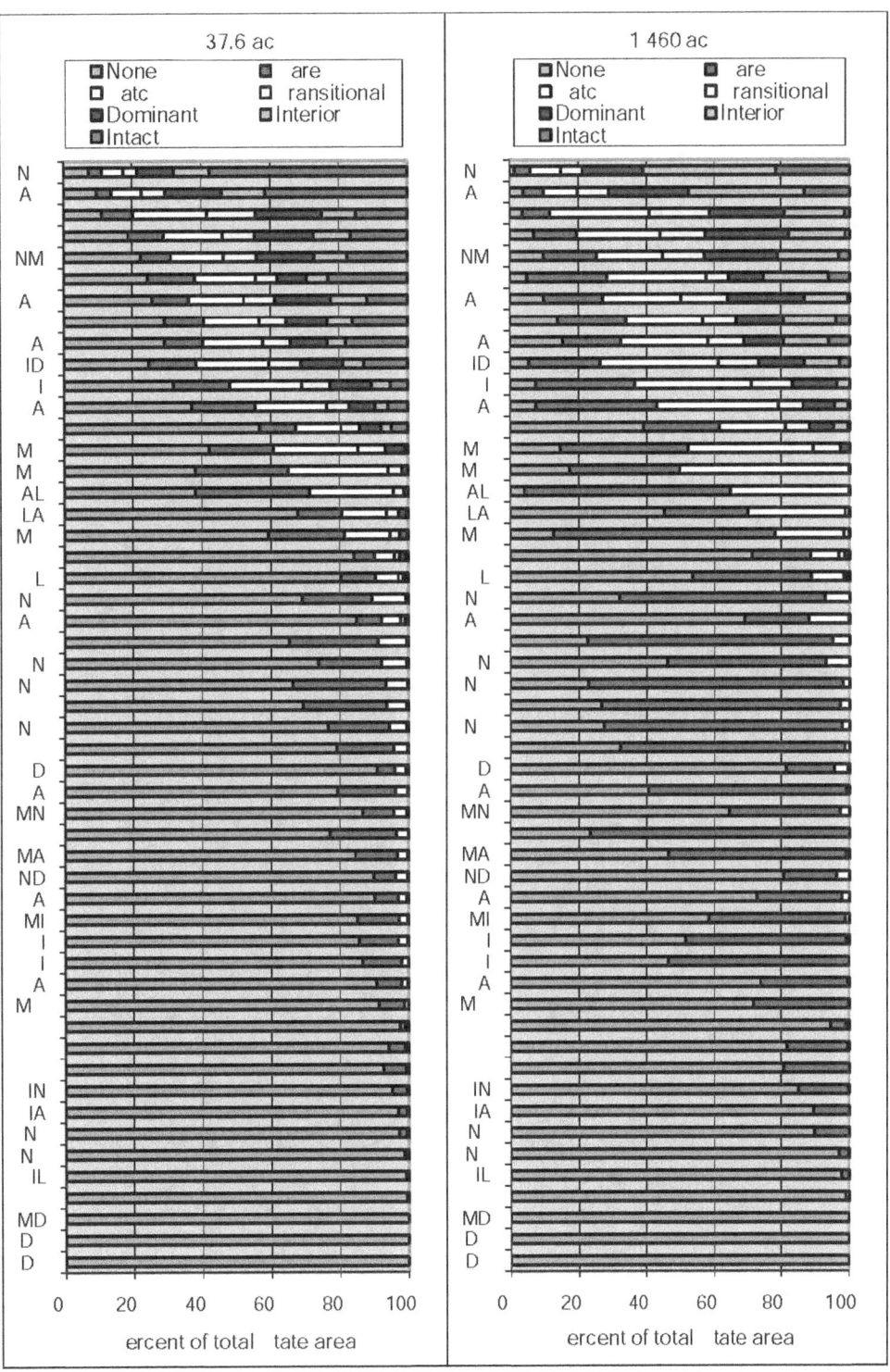

Figure 15—Percent of total State area in seven shrubland area density classes for neighborhood sizes of 37.6 acres (left) and 1,460 acres (right). States are sorted in descending order by percent shrubland (see fig. 5).

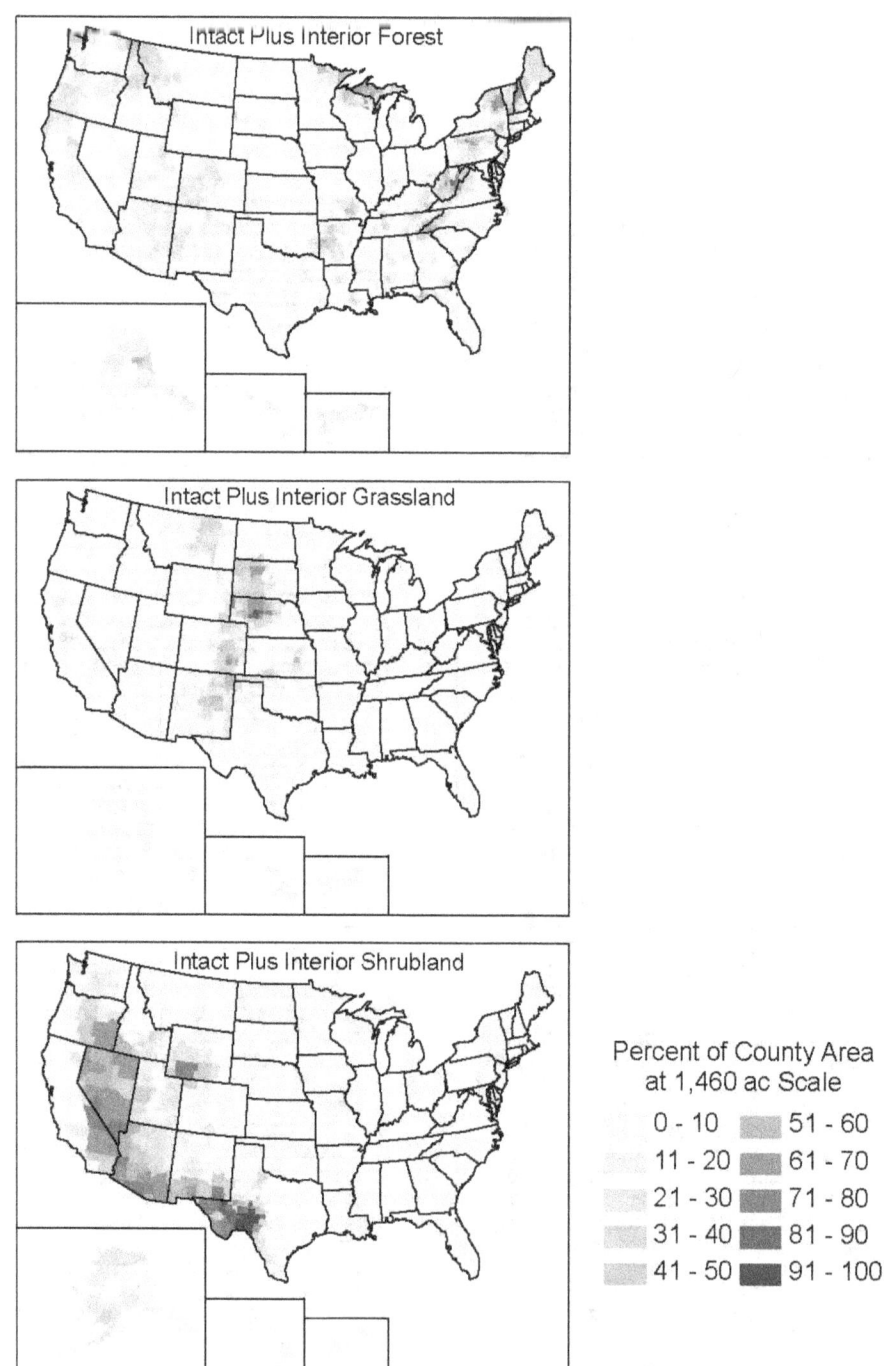

Figure 16—Percent of total county area in both the intact or interior area density classes in 1,460-acre neighborhoods for forest area density (top), grassland area density (middle), and shrubland area density (bottom).

Table 9—Landscape mosaic background, landscape level. Percent of total area in four landscape background classes, for six neighborhood sizes, by Forest and Rangeland Renewable Resources Planning Act of 1974 (RPA) region and national

Neighborhood size	Region	Natural	Agricultural	Developed	Mixed
		---------------------Percent---------------------			
10.9 acres	Alaska	99.9	0.0	0.0	0.0
	North	84.1	10.5	3.0	2.4
	Pacific Coast	79.9	16.3	0.6	3.1
	Rocky Mountain	67.5	20.2	3.4	9.0
	South	46.9	39.2	4.5	9.4
	National	74.5	18.3	2.1	5.1
37.6 acres	Alaska	99.9	0.0	0.0	0.0
	North	45.9	38.8	4.0	11.4
	Pacific Coast	84.2	10.4	2.7	2.7
	Rocky Mountain	79.6	16.1	0.5	3.7
	South	67.1	18.7	3.0	11.3
	National	74.1	17.8	1.9	6.3
162 acres	Alaska	99.9	0.0	0.0	0.0
	North	44.6	37.7	3.5	14.2
	Pacific Coast	84.1	10.1	2.5	3.4
	Rocky Mountain	79.1	15.5	0.5	4.9
	South	66.8	16.2	2.6	14.4
	National	73.7	16.7	1.7	7.9
1,460 acres	Alaska	100.0	0.0	0.0	0.0
	North	43.3	36.2	2.8	17.8
	Pacific Coast	84.0	9.3	2.1	4.6
	Rocky Mountain	78.7	14.1	0.3	6.8
	South	67.4	12.6	2.0	18.0
	National	73.4	15.1	1.3	10.2
13,100 acres	Alaska	100.0	0.0	0.0	0.0
	North	42.6	35.3	2.0	20.2
	Pacific Coast	84.3	8.2	1.6	5.9
	Rocky Mountain	78.9	12.6	0.2	8.3
	South	68.5	9.9	1.3	20.3
	National	73.6	13.7	0.9	11.8
118,000 acres	Alaska	100.0	0.0	0.0	0.0
	North	42.9	34.8	1.1	21.2
	Pacific Coast	85.2	6.5	0.9	7.5
	Rocky Mountain	79.2	11.2	0.1	9.5
	South	69.5	7.1	0.6	22.9
	National	74.1	12.3	0.5	13.1

Rows may not add up to 100 due to rounding off the figures.

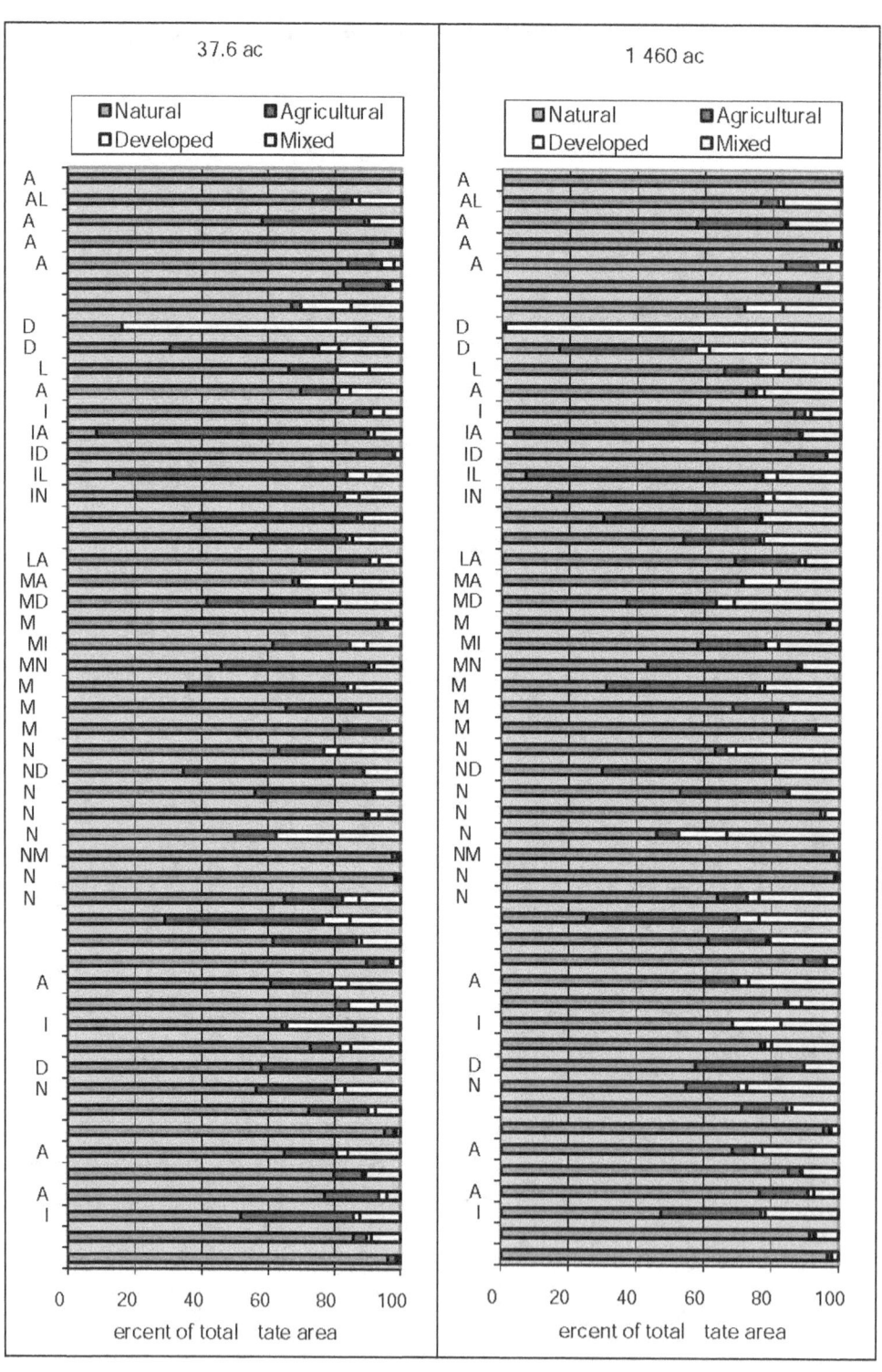

Figure 17—Percent of total State area in four landscape background classes for neighborhood sizes of 37.6 acres (left) and 1,460 acres (right). States are sorted alphabetically.

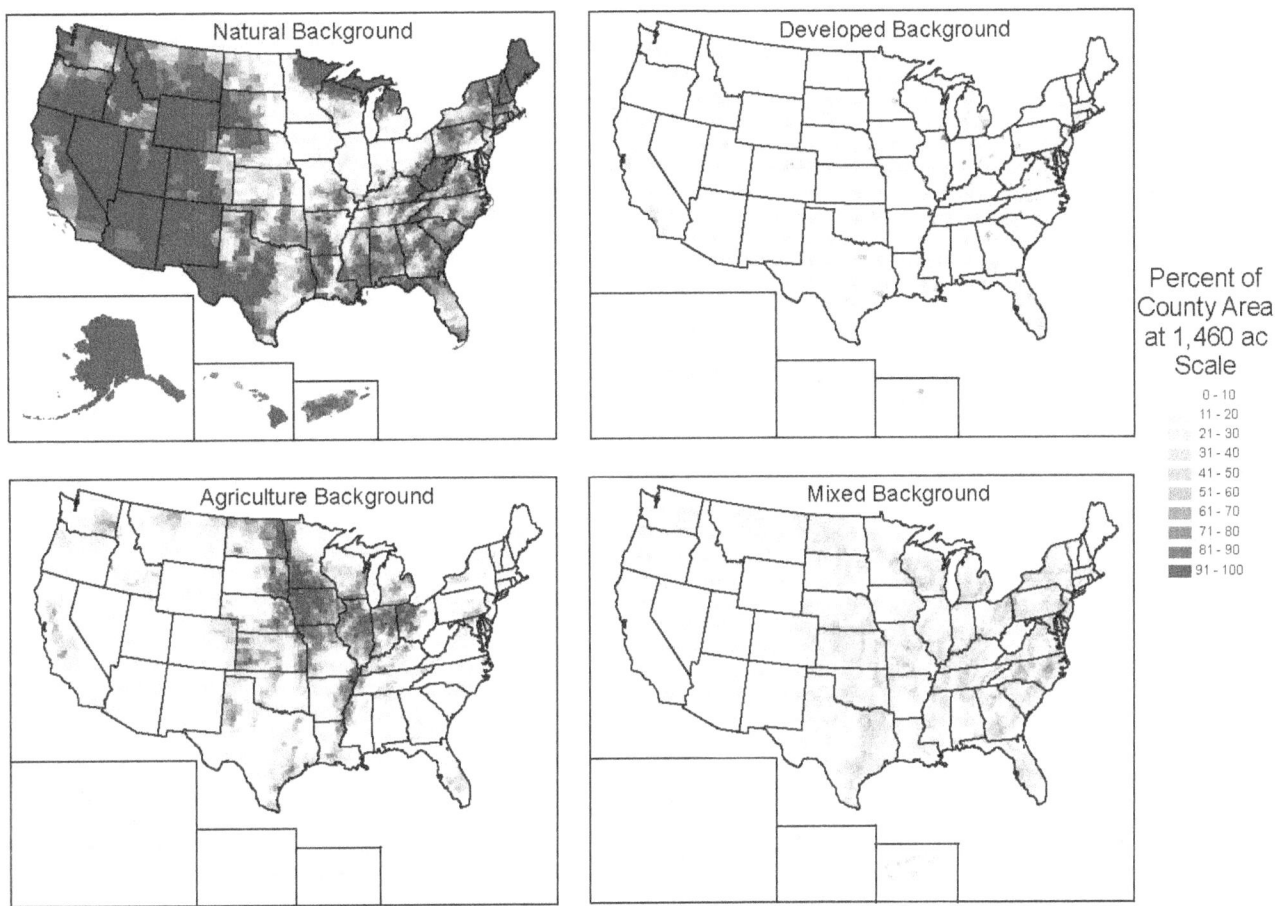

Figure 18—Percent of total county area in the natural, agriculture, developed, and mixed landscape background classes for a 1,460-acre neighborhood size.

Table 10—Forest area density, forest sector level. Percent of total forest area in six forest area density classes, for six neighborhood sizes, by Forest and Rangeland Renewable Resources Planning Act of 1974 (RPA) region and national

Neighborhood size	Region	Rare	Patchy	Transitional	Dominant	Interior	Intact
				----------------------Percent----------------------			
10.9 acres	Alaska	0.0	6.2	8.6	22.6	14.2	48.2
	North	0.0	4.4	8.4	25.0	14.1	48.0
	Pacific Coast	0.0	4.1	7.5	25.1	15.4	47.8
	Rocky Mountain	0.0	7.1	9.2	22.7	13.7	47.3
	South	0.0	5.1	9.9	27.5	14.8	42.6
	National	0.0	5.4	9.0	25.0	14.4	46.2
37.6 acres	Alaska	0.7	7.3	9.8	28.7	22.9	30.7
	North	0.5	6.7	10.5	31.3	23.2	27.8
	Pacific Coast	0.4	5.3	8.9	32.5	25.6	27.3
	Rocky Mountain	1.1	9.1	10.3	28.2	21.9	29.4
	South	0.5	7.5	12.4	34.9	22.4	22.3
	National	0.6	7.3	10.8	31.6	22.9	26.8
162 acres	Alaska	1.2	8.6	11.6	34.7	31.0	12.9
	North	1.0	9.6	12.9	37.3	29.8	9.6
	Pacific Coast	0.7	6.5	10.5	40.5	32.8	9.0
	Rocky Mountain	2.3	11.0	11.6	33.6	29.9	11.7
	South	0.8	10.0	16.1	42.3	24.3	6.5
	National	1.2	9.5	13.2	38.1	28.6	9.5
1,460 acres	Alaska	1.7	10.7	15.1	42.5	29.0	1.0
	North	1.4	13.1	15.5	44.1	25.4	0.5
	Pacific Coast	1.0	7.8	12.7	51.3	26.8	0.4
	Rocky Mountain	3.7	12.9	13.8	41.1	27.9	0.7
	South	1.1	12.5	21.4	50.4	14.1	0.4
	National	1.7	12.0	16.7	46.0	23.0	0.6
13,100 acres	Alaska	2.1	13.9	18.8	47.3	17.9	0.0
	North	1.6	15.4	16.7	50.1	16.2	0.0
	Pacific Coast	1.2	9.2	15.8	60.2	13.6	0.0
	Rocky Mountain	5.0	14.8	18.1	46.9	15.3	0.0
	South	1.2	13.6	25.8	53.3	6.1	0.0
	National	2.1	13.9	20.0	51.1	12.9	0.0
118,000 acres	Alaska	2.4	18.0	22.7	48.6	8.2	0.0
	North	1.8	17.1	17.8	54.9	8.5	0.0
	Pacific Coast	1.1	12.5	20.1	62.7	3.6	0.0
	Rocky Mountain	6.3	20.1	24.9	43.9	4.9	0.0
	South	1.2	14.5	30.3	52.1	1.9	0.0
	National	2.4	16.5	23.9	51.9	5.3	0.0

Rows may not add up to 100 due to rounding off the figures.

Table 11—Grassland area density, grassland sector level. Percent of total grassland area in six grassland area density classes, for six neighborhood sizes, by Forest and Rangeland Renewable Resources Planning Act of 1974 (RPA) region and national

Neighborhood size	Region	Rare	Patchy	Transitional	Dominant	Interior	Intact
				----------Percent----------			
10.9 acres	Alaska	0.1	18.8	17.7	29.1	12.2	22.1
	North	0.5	50.2	24.4	18.4	3.5	2.9
	Pacific Coast	0.1	16.7	17.2	29.9	11.9	24.3
	Rocky Mountain	0.0	7.8	10.3	23.8	11.5	46.5
	South	0.4	19.9	17.5	29.1	10.4	22.7
	National	0.1	12.7	13.0	25.5	11.2	37.5
37.6 acres	Alaska	3.0	21.9	18.9	32.4	13.7	10.1
	North	16.0	55.2	16.7	10.1	1.5	0.4
	Pacific Coast	2.9	21.5	18.3	30.8	14.1	12.4
	Rocky Mountain	1.0	9.8	11.6	27.6	19.4	30.6
	South	4.1	24.0	18.6	29.9	12.8	10.7
	National	2.3	15.4	14.1	28.2	16.9	23.2
162 acres	Alaska	5.3	25.5	20.8	33.4	11.9	2.9
	North	35.4	51.3	9.0	3.9	0.3	0.0
	Pacific Coast	6.0	26.9	18.8	29.4	14.7	4.3
	Rocky Mountain	1.8	12.3	13.9	31.7	26.1	14.4
	South	7.4	29.0	19.6	29.1	11.6	3.3
	National	4.3	18.4	15.7	30.5	20.8	10.3
1,460 acres	Alaska	8.1	31.1	22.9	30.9	6.8	0.2
	North	58.2	38.5	2.4	0.9	0.0	0.0
	Pacific Coast	10.9	32.3	18.8	26.8	11.0	0.2
	Rocky Mountain	2.5	16.5	17.3	36.2	25.3	2.1
	South	11.6	33.7	20.7	27.2	6.3	0.4
	National	6.7	22.5	18.1	32.6	18.6	1.4
13,100 acres	Alaska	10.3	35.4	24.0	27.0	3.3	0.0
	North	69.8	29.4	0.7	0.1	0.0	0.0
	Pacific Coast	15.2	37.0	19.9	22.9	5.0	0.0
	Rocky Mountain	3.0	20.3	20.5	38.4	17.8	0.0
	South	14.5	35.0	23.1	25.1	2.2	0.0
	National	8.3	25.6	20.7	33.0	12.4	0.0
118,000 acres	Alaska	12.7	39.5	24.0	22.1	1.7	0.0
	North	79.2	20.8	0.0	0.0	0.0	0.0
	Pacific Coast	19.7	43.4	21.3	15.3	0.4	0.0
	Rocky Mountain	3.4	23.4	24.0	38.9	10.3	0.0
	South	16.3	36.4	25.4	21.8	0.2	0.0
	National	9.6	28.3	23.4	31.8	6.8	0.0

Rows may not add up to 100 due to rounding off the figures.

Table 12—Shrubland area density, shrubland sector level. Percent of total shrubland area in six shrubland area density classes, for six neighborhood sizes, by Forest and Rangeland Renewable Resources Planning Act of 1974 (RPA) region and national

Neighborhood size	Region	Rare	Patchy	Transitional	Dominant	Interior	Intact
				----------------------Percent----------------------			
10.9 acres	Alaska	0.0	5.9	9.2	24.6	15.2	45.2
	North	0.6	55.2	20.8	16.5	3.9	2.8
	Pacific Coast	0.0	7.3	9.3	18.6	9.0	55.8
	Rocky Mountain	0.0	6.0	8.4	18.9	10.2	56.5
	South	0.3	13.0	11.4	21.2	9.8	44.3
	National	0.1	7.6	9.3	20.7	11.3	51.1
37.6 acres	Alaska	0.6	7.1	10.4	30.7	23.5	27.7
	North	21.5	50.9	14.6	10.9	1.8	0.3
	Pacific Coast	0.8	9.8	10.2	20.5	13.8	44.9
	Rocky Mountain	0.6	7.5	9.2	21.9	16.1	44.6
	South	2.7	15.0	11.7	22.7	14.7	33.2
	National	1.1	9.2	10.1	24.2	17.5	38.0
162 acres	Alaska	0.9	8.6	12.3	36.3	30.7	11.1
	North	40.6	44.0	10.0	5.1	0.3	0.0
	Pacific Coast	1.5	12.6	10.9	21.5	21.2	32.3
	Rocky Mountain	1.0	9.0	10.2	24.1	24.7	31.1
	South	4.5	17.8	11.7	22.9	21.1	22.0
	National	1.9	10.9	11.1	26.8	25.1	24.2
1,460 acres	Alaska	1.2	11.3	16.1	41.9	28.4	1.2
	North	59.3	35.8	4.1	0.8	0.0	0.0
	Pacific Coast	2.3	16.0	11.7	23.4	33.6	13.1
	Rocky Mountain	1.3	11.0	11.4	27.4	36.6	12.2
	South	6.6	20.7	11.1	23.2	30.3	8.2
	National	2.7	13.4	12.6	30.0	32.7	8.6
13,100 acres	Alaska	1.2	15.2	19.7	44.8	19.2	0.0
	North	70.3	28.9	0.8	0.0	0.0	0.0
	Pacific Coast	2.4	18.8	13.4	26.9	37.6	0.9
	Rocky Mountain	1.4	12.7	13.2	33.1	38.4	1.3
	South	7.6	21.4	11.9	24.6	33.6	0.9
	National	3.0	15.6	14.7	34.0	32.0	0.8
118,000 acres	Alaska	1.1	19.3	23.5	46.3	9.8	0.0
	North	78.0	22.0	0.0	0.0	0.0	0.0
	Pacific Coast	2.2	22.1	15.6	31.5	28.6	0.0
	Rocky Mountain	1.3	14.6	15.3	41.3	27.5	0.0
	South	8.0	21.9	13.2	26.3	30.6	0.0
	National	3.0	18.0	17.2	38.8	23.0	0.0

Rows may not add up to 100 due to rounding off the figures.

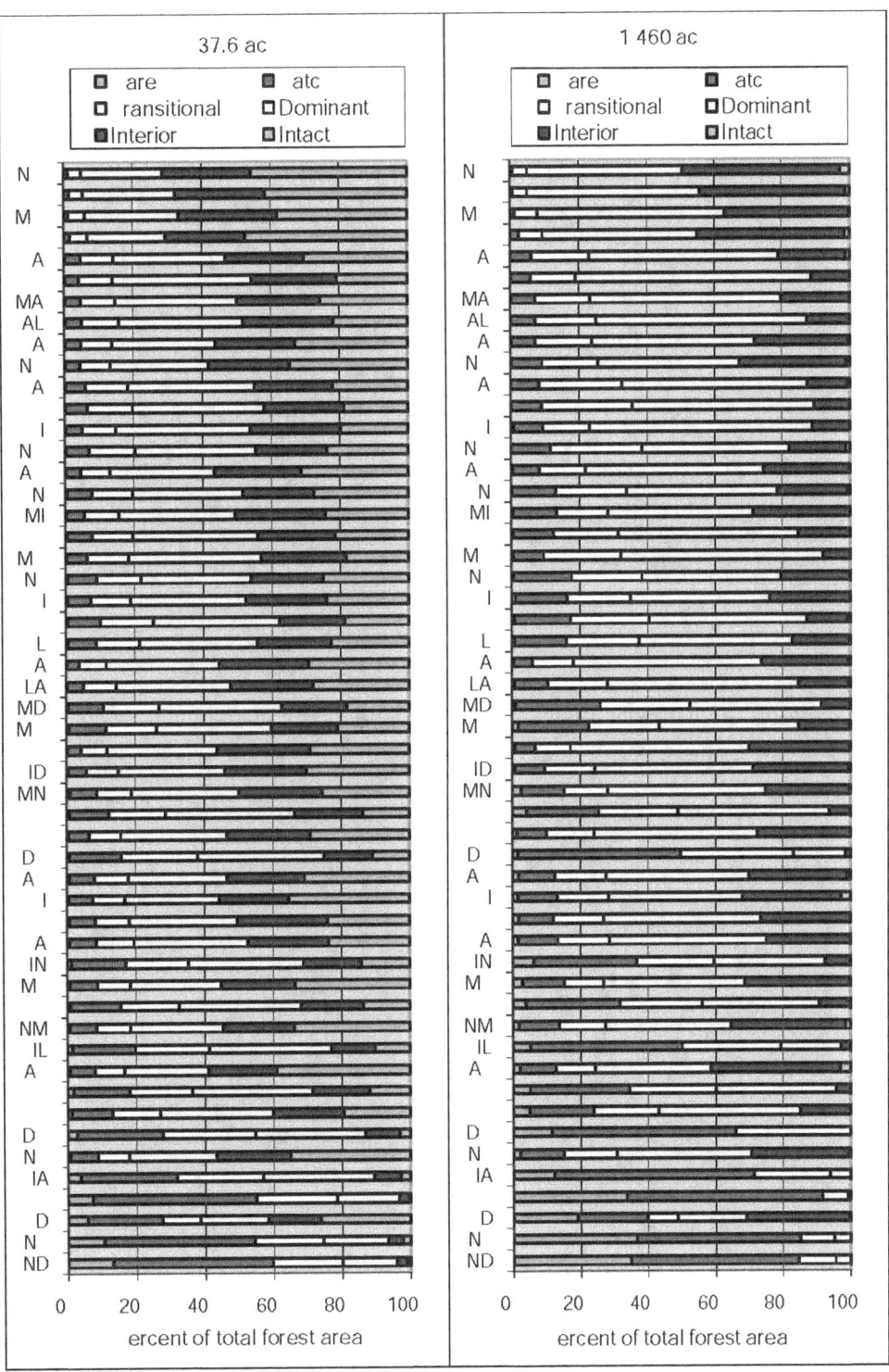

Figure 19—Percent of total forest area in each State in six forest area density classes for neighborhood sizes of 37.6 acres (left) and 1,460 acres (right). States are sorted in descending order by percent forest (fig. 5). Compare to figure 13.

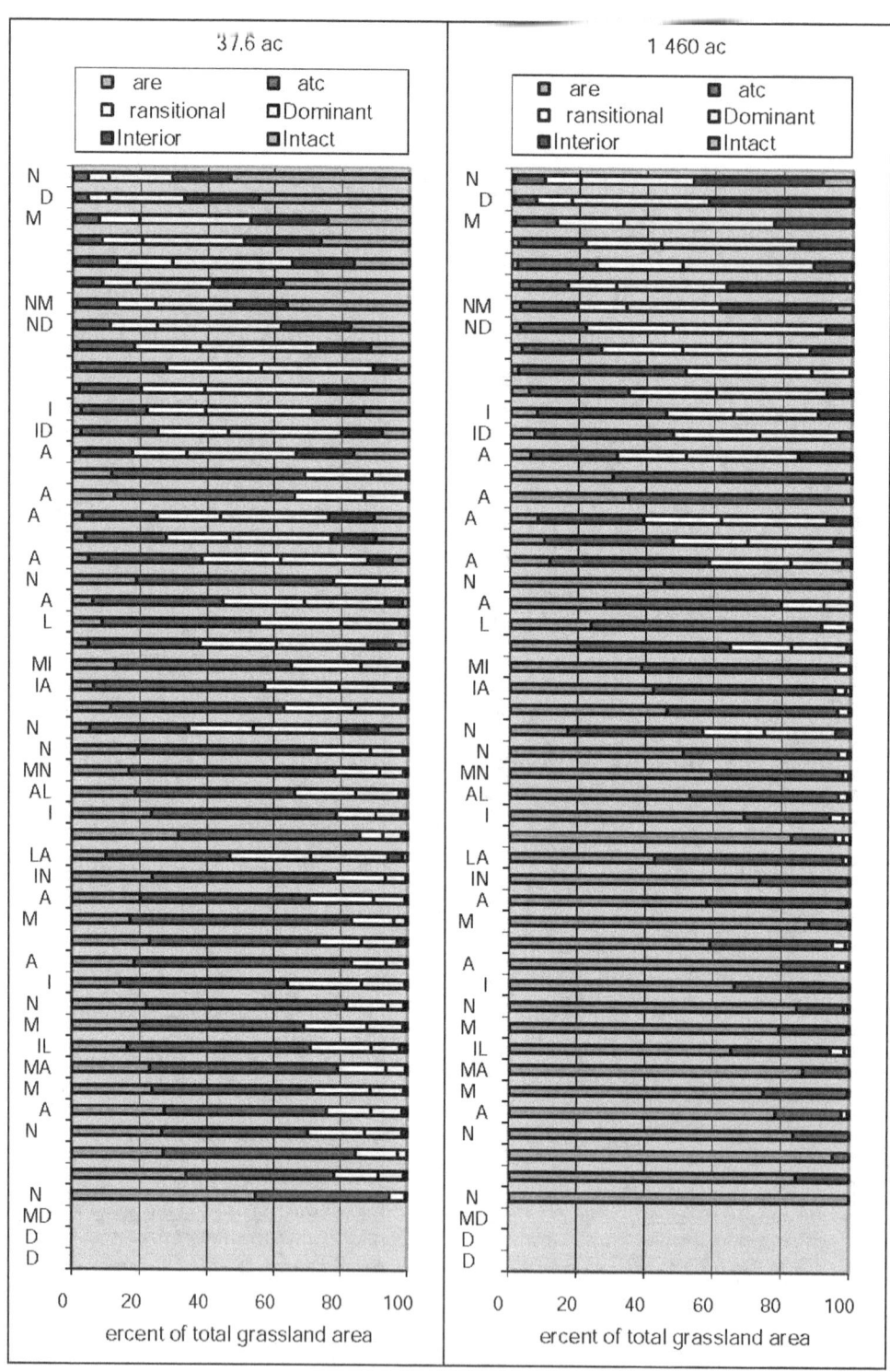

Figure 20—Percent of total grassland area in each State in six grassland area density classes for neighborhood sizes of 37.6 acres (left) and 1,460 acres (right). States are sorted in descending order by percent grassland (fig. 5). Compare to figure 14.

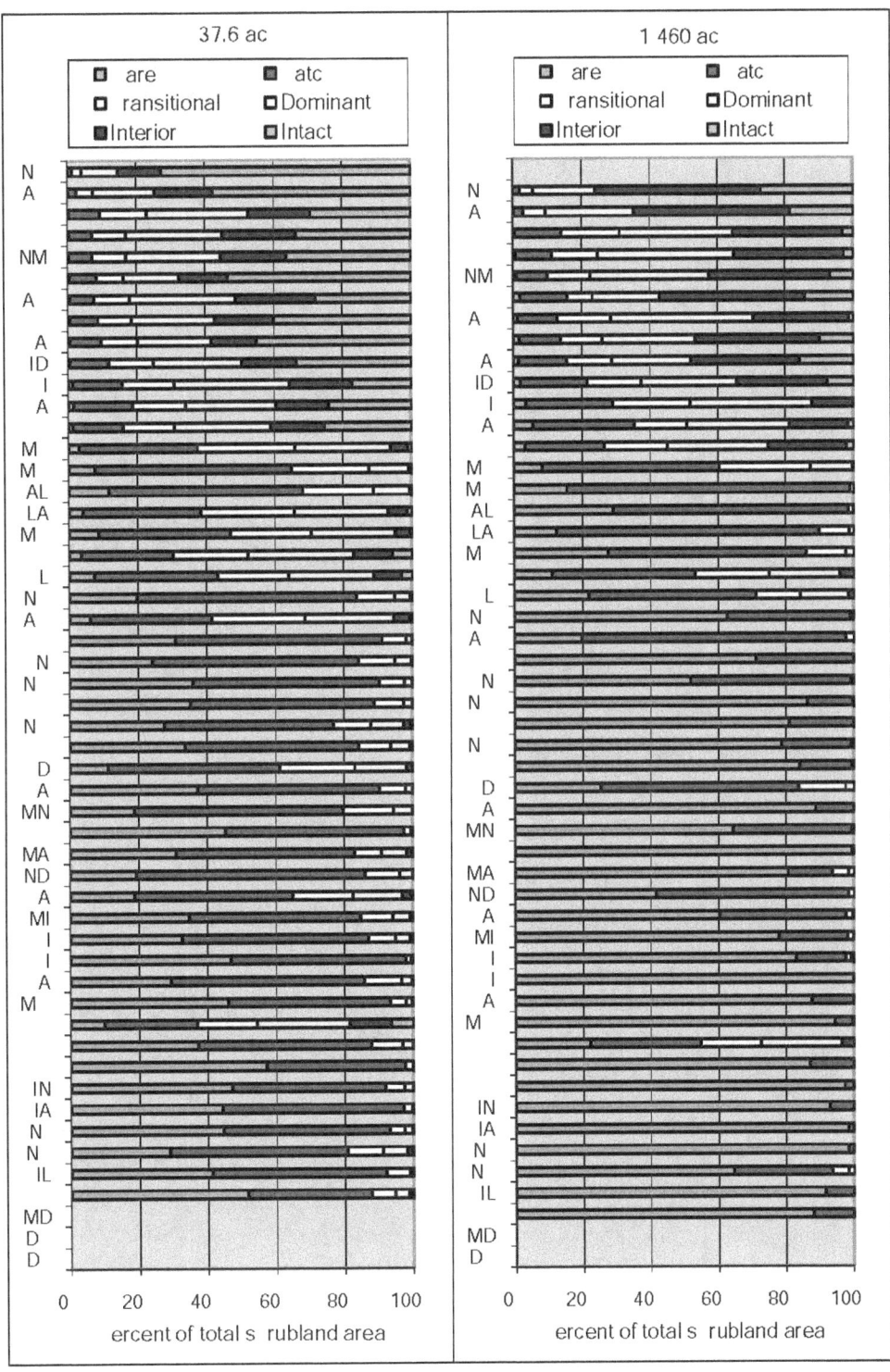

Figure 21—Percent of total shrubland area in each State in six shrubland area density classes for neighborhood sizes of 37.6 acres (left) and 1,460 acres (right). States are sorted in descending order by percent shrubland (fig. 5). Compare to figure 15.

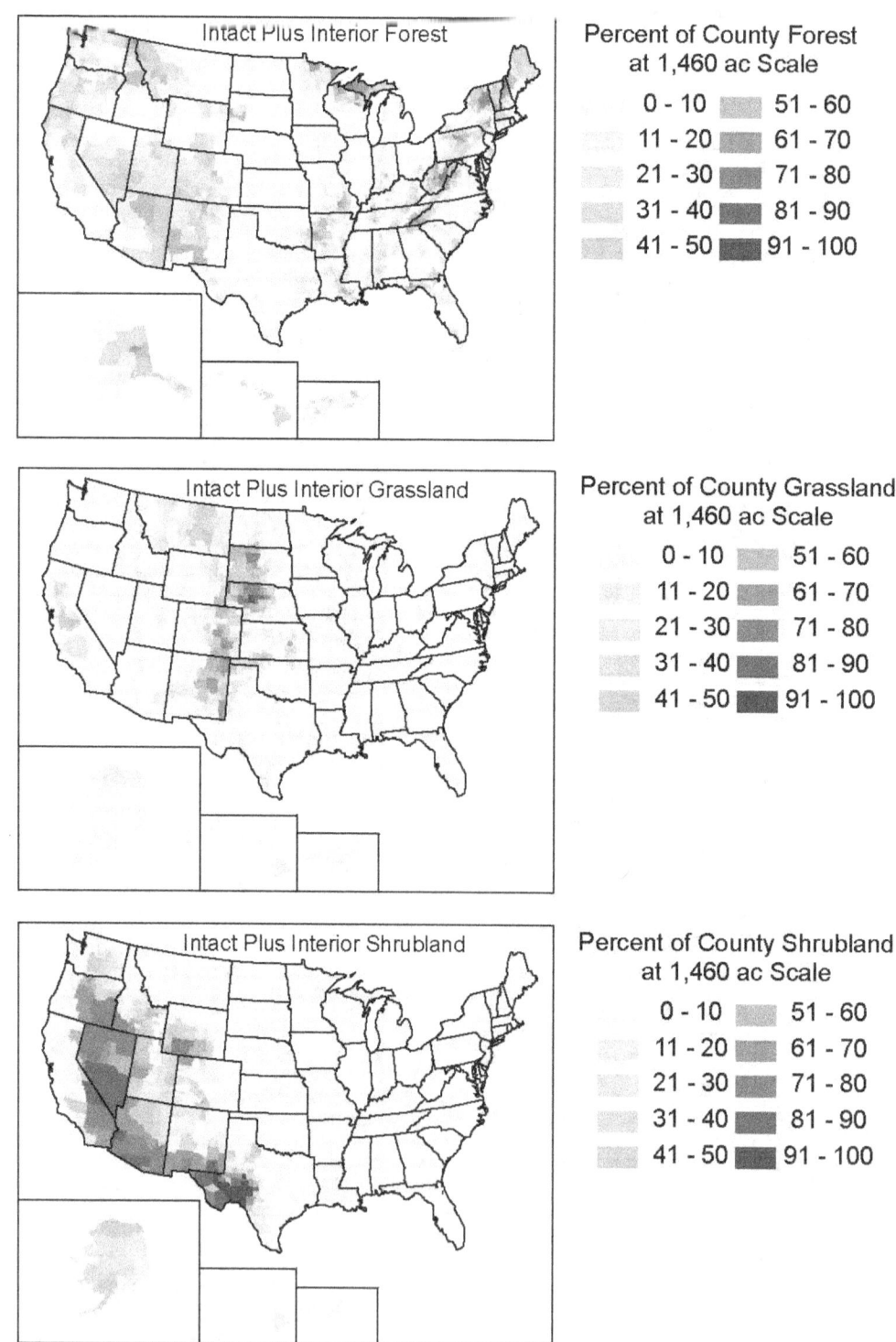

Figure 22—Percent of total forest, grassland, or shrubland area in the intact or interior area density classes in 1,460-acre neighborhoods for forest area density (top), grassland area density (middle), and shrubland area density (bottom). Compare to figure 16.

Table 13—Landscape mosaic background, forest sector level. Percent of total forest area in four background classes, for six neighborhood sizes, by Forest and Rangeland Renewable Resources Planning Act of 1974 (RPA) region and national

Neighborhood size	Region	Natural	Agricultural	Developed	Mixed
			-----------------Percent-----------------		
10.9 acres	Alaska	100.0	0.0	0.0	0.0
	North	91.1	1.9	0.2	6.8
	Pacific Coast	99.1	0.1	0.1	0.7
	Rocky Mountain	98.4	0.5	0.0	1.0
	South	93.6	1.0	0.3	5.1
	National	95.3	0.9	0.2	3.6
37.6 acres	Alaska	100.0	0.0	0.0	0.0
	North	87.4	3.4	0.4	8.9
	Pacific Coast	98.9	0.1	0.1	0.8
	Rocky Mountain	98.0	0.8	0.0	1.2
	South	90.9	1.7	0.4	7.1
	National	93.4	1.6	0.2	4.8
162 acres	Alaska	100.0	0.0	0.0	0.0
	North	82.8	5.1	0.5	11.7
	Pacific Coast	98.6	0.2	0.2	1.0
	Rocky Mountain	97.5	1.1	0.0	1.4
	South	87.5	2.4	0.5	9.7
	National	91.1	2.3	0.3	6.4
1,460 acres	Alaska	100.0	0.0	0.0	0.0
	North	77.4	6.9	0.6	15.1
	Pacific Coast	98.3	0.3	0.2	1.2
	Rocky Mountain	96.9	1.3	0.0	1.7
	South	83.9	2.6	0.5	13.1
	National	88.4	2.9	0.3	8.4
13,100 acres	Alaska	100.0	0.0	0.0	0.0
	North	74.7	7.9	0.5	17.0
	Pacific Coast	98.2	0.3	0.1	1.4
	Rocky Mountain	96.7	1.5	0.0	1.8
	South	82.2	2.4	0.4	15.0
	National	87.2	3.1	0.3	9.5
118,000 acres	Alaska	100.0	0.0	0.0	0.0
	North	73.8	8.6	0.3	17.4
	Pacific Coast	98.3	0.2	0.1	1.4
	Rocky Mountain	96.7	1.5	0.0	1.8
	South	81.1	1.9	0.1	16.8
	National	86.6	3.1	0.1	10.2

Rows may not add up to 100 due to rounding off the figures.

Table 14—Landscape mosaic background, grassland sector level. Percent of total grassland area in four background classes, for six neighborhood sizes, by Forest and Rangeland Renewable Resources Planning Act of 1974 (RPA) region and national

Neighborhood size	Region	Natural	Agricultural	Developed	Mixed
			-----------------Percent-----------------		
10.9 acres	Alaska	100.0	0.0	0.0	0.0
	North	69.4	10.8	0.5	19.3
	Pacific Coast	96.1	0.7	0.4	2.8
	Rocky Mountain	95.5	1.3	0.0	3.2
	South	90.4	2.0	0.2	7.4
	National	94.3	1.5	0.1	4.1
37.6 acres	Alaska	100.0	0.0	0.0	0.0
	North	63.2	15.5	0.7	20.7
	Pacific Coast	95.2	0.9	0.6	3.3
	Rocky Mountain	94.0	1.9	0.0	4.0
	South	88.2	2.7	0.3	8.9
	National	92.7	2.2	0.1	5.0
162 acres	Alaska	100.0	0.0	0.0	0.0
	North	55.9	20.3	0.8	23.0
	Pacific Coast	94.0	1.2	0.6	4.1
	Rocky Mountain	91.6	2.8	0.0	5.6
	South	85.4	3.3	0.3	11.0
	National	90.4	3.0	0.1	6.5
1,460 acres	Alaska	100.0	0.0	0.0	0.0
	North	47.7	26.7	0.8	24.8
	Pacific Coast	91.9	1.7	0.7	5.8
	Rocky Mountain	87.4	4.3	0.0	8.3
	South	81.9	3.8	0.2	14.0
	National	86.7	4.3	0.1	8.9
13,100 acres	Alaska	100.0	0.0	0.0	0.0
	North	43.8	31.0	0.7	24.5
	Pacific Coast	89.8	2.0	0.6	7.6
	Rocky Mountain	84.5	5.0	0.0	10.5
	South	80.4	3.7	0.2	15.8
	National	84.3	4.8	0.1	10.8
118,000 acres	Alaska	100.0	0.0	0.0	0.0
	North	42.9	34.9	0.5	21.7
	Pacific Coast	88.0	2.1	0.3	9.7
	Rocky Mountain	82.2	5.0	0.0	12.9
	South	79.7	2.9	0.1	17.3
	National	82.6	4.8	0.0	12.6

Rows may not add up to 100 due to rounding off the figures.

Table 15—Landscape mosaic background, shrubland sector level. Percent of total shrubland area in four background classes, for six neighborhood sizes, by Forest and Rangeland Renewable Resources Planning Act of 1974 (RPA) region and national

Neighborhood size	Region	Natural	Agricultural	Developed	Mixed
			------------------Percent------------------		
10.9 acres	Alaska	100.0	0.0	0.0	0.0
	North	86.2	4.3	0.2	9.3
	Pacific Coast	98.8	0.2	0.1	1.0
	Rocky Mountain	99.4	0.1	0.0	0.5
	South	95.0	1.2	0.1	3.8
	National	98.7	0.3	0.0	1.0
37.6 acres	Alaska	100.0	0.0	0.0	0.0
	North	83.4	5.7	0.3	10.6
	Pacific Coast	98.5	0.4	0.1	1.1
	Rocky Mountain	99.3	0.1	0.0	0.5
	South	94.0	1.5	0.1	4.3
	National	98.5	0.4	0.0	1.1
162 acres	Alaska	100.0	0.0	0.0	0.0
	North	80.8	6.8	0.3	12.0
	Pacific Coast	98.0	0.5	0.1	1.4
	Rocky Mountain	99.1	0.2	0.0	0.6
	South	93.0	1.7	0.1	5.2
	National	98.2	0.5	0.0	1.3
1,460 acres	Alaska	100.0	0.0	0.0	0.0
	North	78.5	7.2	0.4	13.9
	Pacific Coast	97.2	0.7	0.1	1.9
	Rocky Mountain	98.9	0.2	0.0	0.9
	South	91.7	1.8	0.1	6.4
	National	97.8	0.5	0.0	1.7
13,100 acres	Alaska	100.0	0.0	0.0	0.0
	North	77.6	6.7	0.3	15.3
	Pacific Coast	96.4	0.9	0.1	2.6
	Rocky Mountain	98.9	0.2	0.0	0.9
	South	91.2	1.6	0.0	7.2
	National	97.6	0.5	0.0	1.9
118,000 acres	Alaska	100.0	0.0	0.0	0.0
	North	78.1	6.5	0.1	15.2
	Pacific Coast	95.6	0.8	0.1	3.5
	Rocky Mountain	99.1	0.1	0.0	0.8
	South	90.5	0.9	0.0	8.5
	National	97.5	0.3	0.0	2.2

Rows may not add up to 100 due to rounding off the figures.

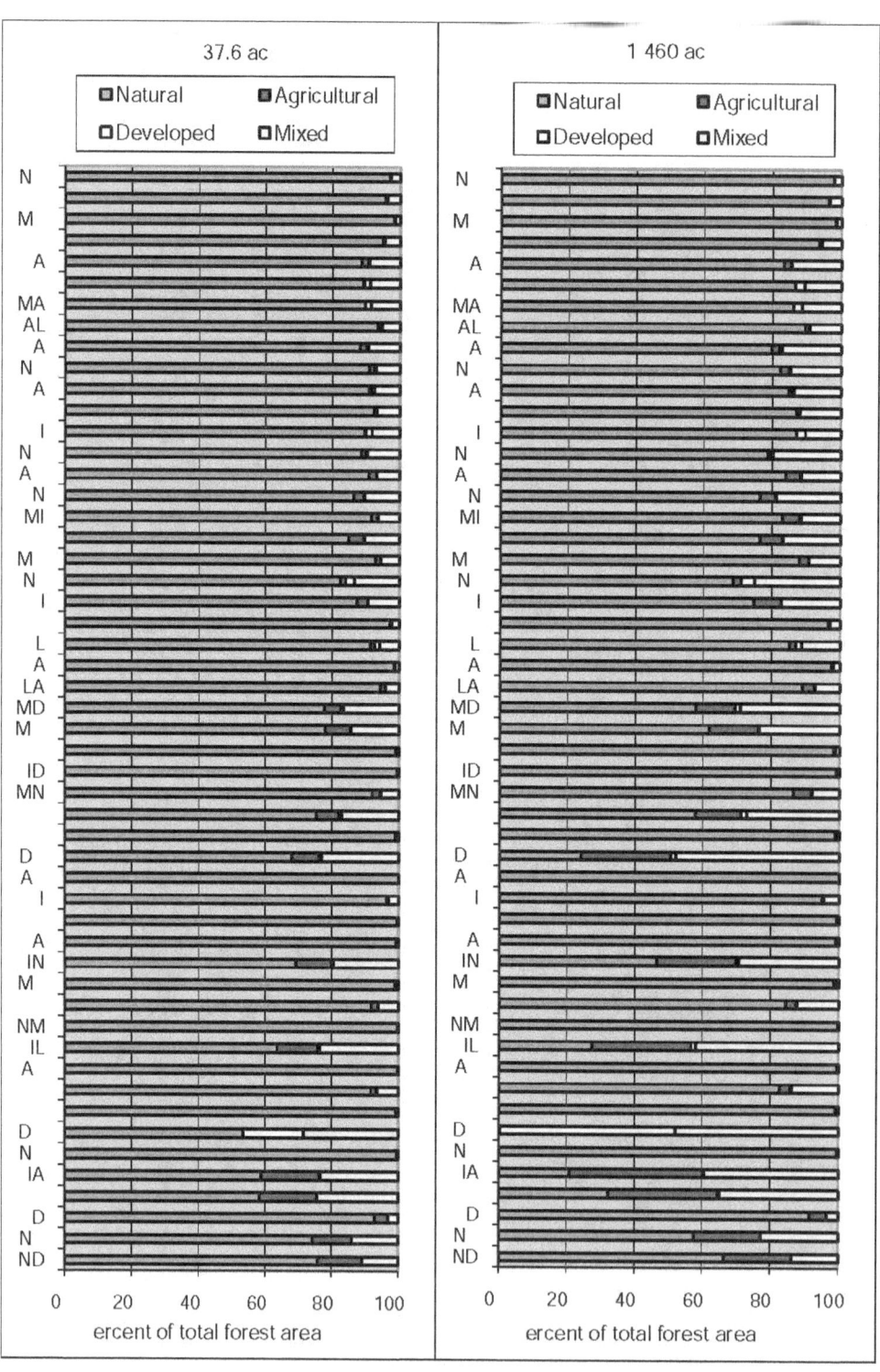

Figure 23—Percent of total forest area in each State in four landscape background classes for neighborhood sizes of 37.6 acres (left) and 1,460 acres (right). States are sorted in descending order by percent forest (fig. 5). Compare to figure 18.

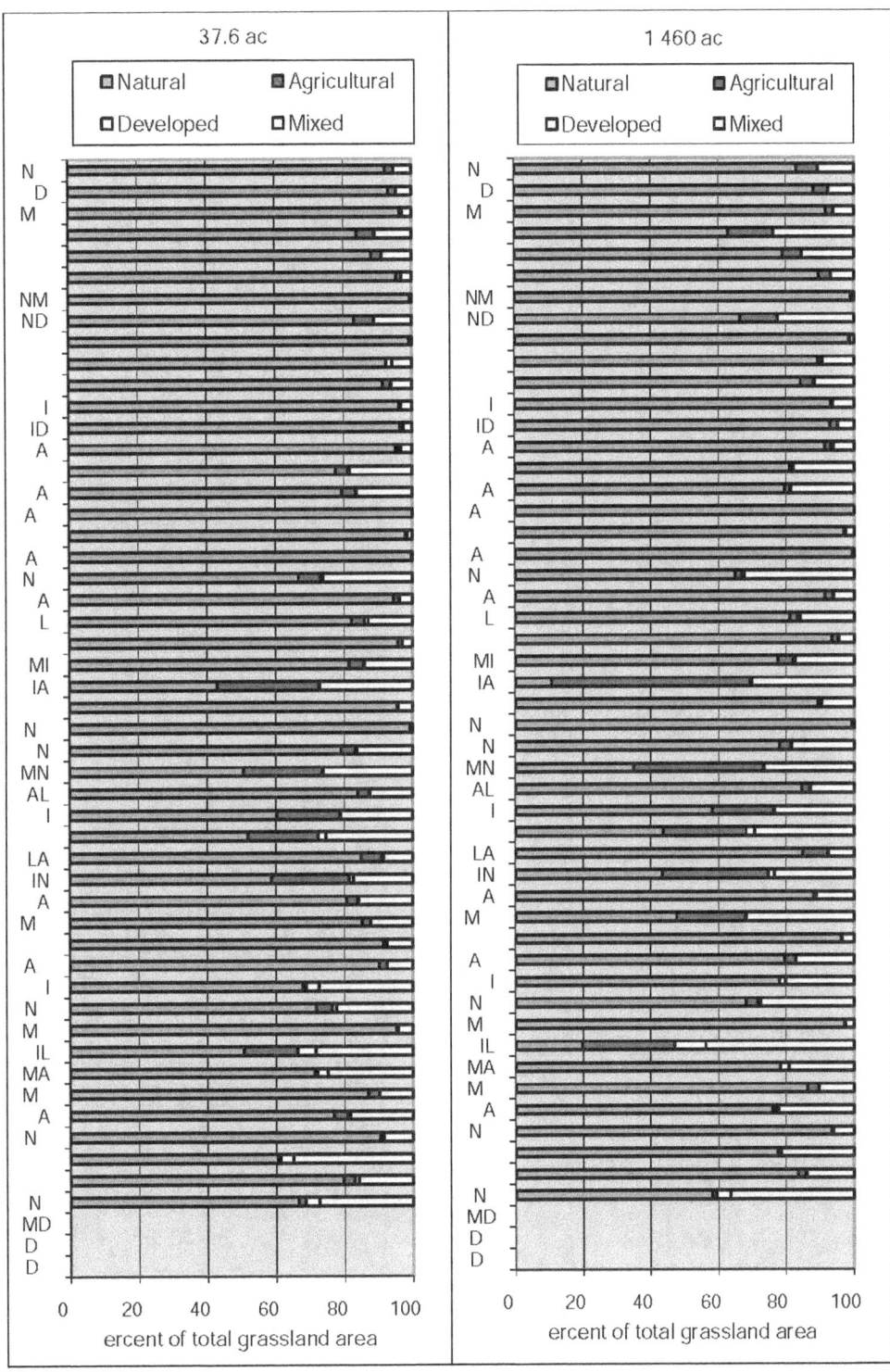

Figure 24—Percent of total grassland area in each State in four landscape background classes for neighborhood sizes of 37.6 acres (left) and 1,460 acres (right). States are sorted in descending order by percent grassland (fig. 5). Compare to figure 18.

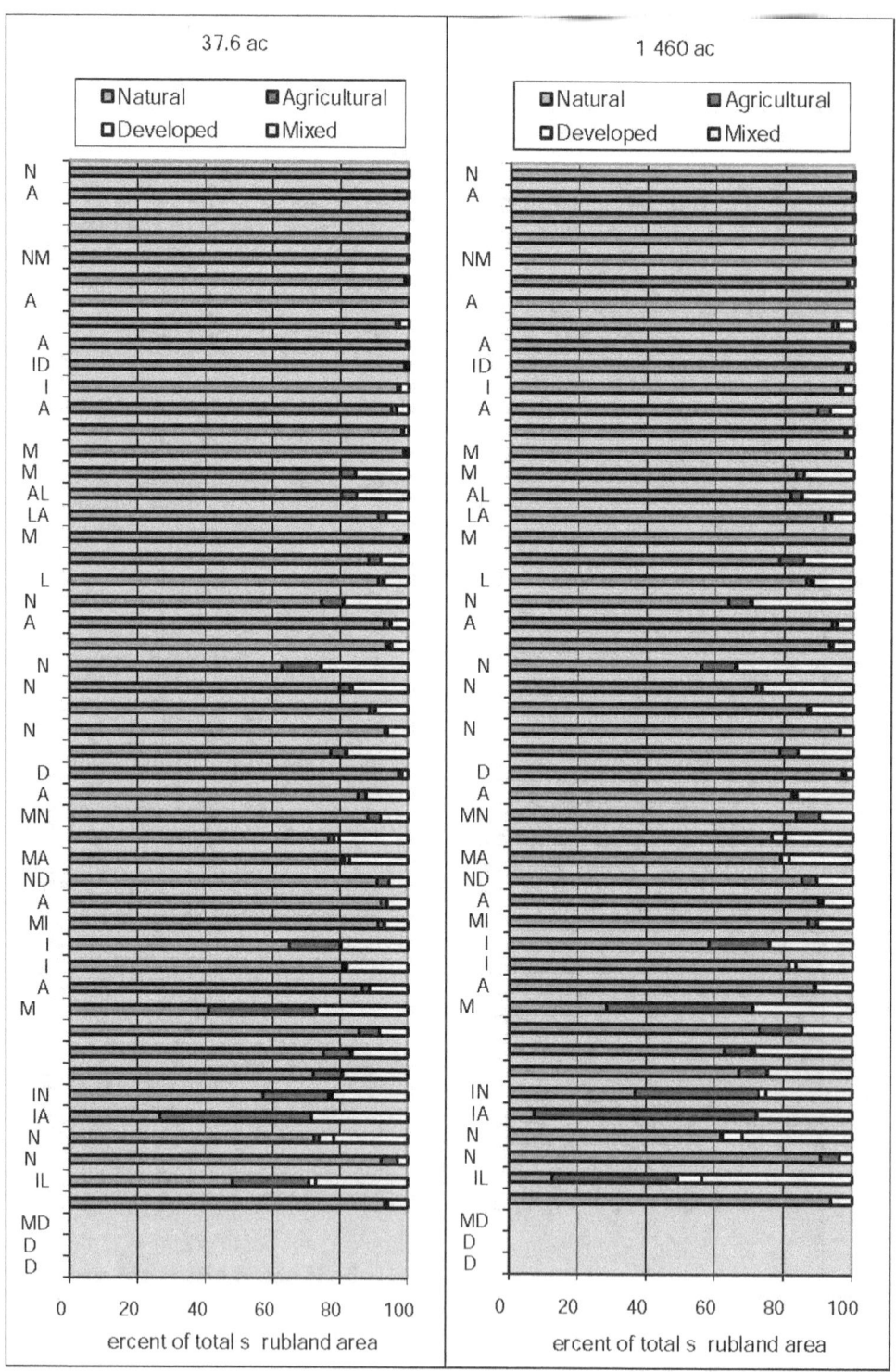

Figure 25—Percent of total shrubland area in each State in four landscape background classes for neighborhood sizes of 37.6 acres (left) and 1,460 acres (right). States are sorted in descending order by percent shrubland (fig. 5). Compare to figure 18.

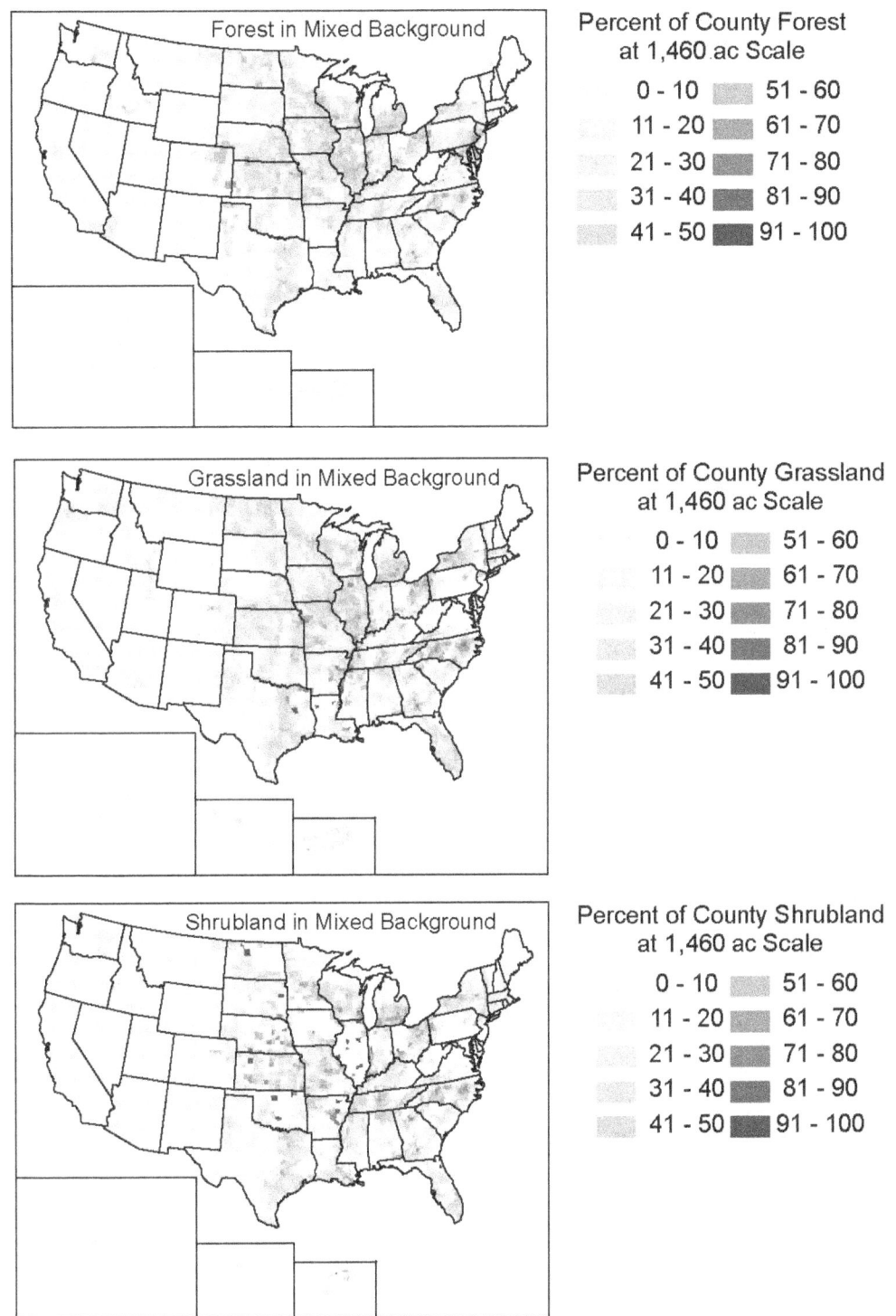

Figure 26—Percent of total county forest (top), grassland (middle), and shrubland (bottom) area in the mixed landscape mosaic background class in 1,460-acre neighborhoods.

Table 16—Landscape mosaic interface zones, forest sector level. Percent of total forest area in three types of developed and three types of agriculture interface classes, for six neighborhood sizes, by Forest and Rangeland Renewable Resources Planning Act of 1974 (RPA) region and national

Neighborhood size	Region	Developed-dominant	Developed-subdominant	Developed-minor	Agriculture-dominant	Agriculture-subdominant	Agriculture-minor
			--------Percent--------			--------Percent--------	
10.9 acres	Alaska	0.0	0.4	99.6	0.0	0.0	100.0
	North	0.2	12.9	86.9	1.9	18.1	80.0
	Pacific Coast	0.1	8.0	91.9	0.1	1.0	98.9
	Rocky Mountain	0.0	1.7	98.3	0.5	2.6	96.8
	South	0.3	12.7	87.0	1.0	16.1	82.9
	National	0.2	8.5	91.4	0.9	10.3	88.8
37.6 acres	Alaska	0.0	0.4	99.6	0.0	0.0	100.0
	North	0.4	12.9	86.7	3.4	23.5	73.2
	Pacific Coast	0.1	7.8	92.1	0.1	1.4	98.4
	Rocky Mountain	0.0	1.7	98.3	0.8	3.0	96.2
	South	0.4	12.5	87.2	1.7	22.3	76.0
	National	0.2	8.3	91.4	1.6	13.7	84.7
162 acres	Alaska	0.0	0.3	99.7	0.0	0.1	99.9
	North	0.5	12.0	87.6	5.1	29.7	65.2
	Pacific Coast	0.2	6.2	93.6	0.2	2.0	97.8
	Rocky Mountain	0.0	1.5	98.5	1.1	3.6	95.3
	South	0.5	11.0	88.5	2.4	31.0	66.6
	National	0.3	7.4	92.3	2.3	18.2	79.5
1,460 acres	Alaska	0.0	0.3	99.7	0.0	0.1	99.9
	North	0.6	11.3	88.2	6.9	36.9	56.2
	Pacific Coast	0.2	4.4	95.4	0.3	3.1	96.6
	Rocky Mountain	0.0	1.0	99.0	1.3	4.5	94.2
	South	0.5	9.9	89.6	2.6	43.6	53.8
	National	0.3	6.7	93.0	2.9	24.2	72.9
13,100 acres	Alaska	0.0	0.3	99.7	0.0	0.1	99.9
	North	0.5	12.3	87.3	7.9	41.3	50.8
	Pacific Coast	0.1	4.6	95.3	0.3	4.4	95.3
	Rocky Mountain	0.0	0.9	99.1	1.5	5.4	93.2
	South	0.4	11.3	88.4	2.4	54.0	43.7
	National	0.3	7.3	92.4	3.1	28.9	68.1
118,000 acres	Alaska	0.0	0.2	99.8	0.0	0.1	99.9
	North	0.3	13.7	86.0	8.6	45.4	46.0
	Pacific Coast	0.1	5.4	94.6	0.2	6.5	93.2
	Rocky Mountain	0.0	0.9	99.0	1.5	7.1	91.3
	South	0.1	13.0	86.8	1.9	63.7	34.4
	National	0.1	8.3	91.5	3.1	33.5	63.4

Rows may not add up to 100 due to rounding off the figures.

Table 17—Landscape mosaic interface zones, grassland sector level. Percent of total grassland area in three types of developed and three types of agriculture interface classes, for six neighborhood sizes, by Forest and Rangeland Renewable Resources Planning Act of 1974 (RPA) region and national

Neighborhood size	Region	Developed-dominant	Developed-subdominant	Developed-minor	Agriculture-dominant	Agriculture-subdominant	Agriculture-minor
		--------Percent--------			--------Percent--------		
10.9 acres	Alaska	0.0	0.1	99.9	0.0	0.0	100.0
	North	0.5	27.9	71.7	10.8	35.5	53.7
	Pacific Coast	0.4	13.0	86.5	0.7	4.7	94.6
	Rocky Mountain	0.0	6.7	93.2	1.3	8.6	90.2
	South	0.2	16.4	83.3	2.0	17.9	80.1
	National	0.1	8.9	91.0	1.5	10.1	88.4
37.6 acres	Alaska	0.0	0.1	99.9	0.0	0.0	100.0
	North	0.7	25.8	73.5	15.5	39.9	44.6
	Pacific Coast	0.6	13.2	86.2	0.9	6.5	92.6
	Rocky Mountain	0.0	4.3	95.7	1.9	11.9	86.2
	South	0.3	13.4	86.3	2.7	23.1	74.2
	National	0.1	6.7	93.2	2.2	13.4	84.4
162 acres	Alaska	0.0	0.1	99.9	0.0	0.0	100.0
	North	0.8	20.9	78.3	20.3	44.1	35.5
	Pacific Coast	0.6	11.7	87.6	1.2	9.2	89.5
	Rocky Mountain	0.0	2.8	97.2	2.8	17.6	79.6
	South	0.3	10.8	88.9	3.3	31.5	65.2
	National	0.1	5.1	94.8	3.0	18.9	78.1
1,460 acres	Alaska	0.0	0.1	99.9	0.0	0.0	100.0
	North	0.8	16.1	83.1	26.7	44.7	28.6
	Pacific Coast	0.7	10.4	88.9	1.7	14.5	83.8
	Rocky Mountain	0.0	1.2	98.8	4.3	26.4	69.4
	South	0.2	8.4	91.4	3.8	42.6	53.5
	National	0.1	3.4	96.5	4.3	26.9	68.8
13,100 acres	Alaska	0.0	0.0	100.0	0.0	0.0	100.0
	North	0.7	15.9	83.4	31.0	44.0	25.1
	Pacific Coast	0.6	11.4	88.1	2.0	21.1	76.9
	Rocky Mountain	0.0	1.0	99.0	5.0	33.4	61.6
	South	0.2	8.6	91.2	3.7	51.6	44.7
	National	0.1	3.3	96.6	4.8	33.5	61.7
118,000 acres	Alaska	0.0	0.0	100.0	0.0	0.0	100.0
	North	0.5	14.6	84.8	34.9	42.5	22.6
	Pacific Coast	0.3	13.9	85.8	2.1	30.5	67.4
	Rocky Mountain	0.0	0.9	99.1	5.0	39.7	55.3
	South	0.1	9.0	90.9	2.9	60.6	36.5
	National	0.0	3.5	96.5	4.8	39.8	55.4

Rows may not add up to 100 due to rounding off the figures.

Table 18—Landscape mosaic interface zones, shrubland sector level. Percent of total shrubland area in three types of developed and three types of agriculture interface classes, for six neighborhood sizes, by Forest and Rangeland Renewable Resources Planning Act of 1974 (RPA) region and national

Neighborhood size	Region	Developed-dominant	Developed-subdominant	Developed-minor	Agriculture-dominant	Agriculture-subdominant	Agriculture-minor
		--------Percent--------			--------Percent--------		
10.9 acres	Alaska	0.0	0.1	99.9	0.0	0.0	100.0
	North	0.2	13.5	86.3	4.3	21.4	74.3
	Pacific Coast	0.1	5.0	94.9	0.2	1.9	97.9
	Rocky Mountain	0.0	2.2	97.8	0.1	1.3	98.6
	South	0.1	8.4	91.5	1.2	9.9	88.9
	National	0.0	3.0	97.0	0.3	2.4	97.3
37.6 acres	Alaska	0.0	0.1	99.9	0.0	0.0	100.0
	North	0.3	12.6	87.1	5.7	24.0	70.3
	Pacific Coast	0.1	5.0	94.9	0.4	2.6	97.1
	Rocky Mountain	0.0	2.4	97.6	0.1	1.7	98.2
	South	0.1	7.4	92.5	1.5	12.3	86.2
	National	0.0	2.9	97.1	0.4	3.0	96.6
162 acres	Alaska	0.0	0.1	99.9	0.0	0.0	100.0
	North	0.3	10.9	88.7	6.8	26.8	66.4
	Pacific Coast	0.1	4.3	95.6	0.5	3.8	95.6
	Rocky Mountain	0.0	2.0	97.9	0.2	2.4	97.4
	South	0.1	5.6	94.3	1.7	16.0	82.3
	National	0.0	2.4	97.6	0.5	4.1	95.5
1,460 acres	Alaska	0.0	0.0	100.0	0.0	0.0	100.0
	North	0.4	9.1	90.5	7.2	30.6	62.1
	Pacific Coast	0.1	3.3	96.6	0.7	6.3	92.9
	Rocky Mountain	0.0	1.3	98.7	0.2	4.1	95.7
	South	0.1	3.5	96.4	1.8	21.2	76.9
	National	0.0	1.6	98.4	0.5	5.9	93.6
13,100 acres	Alaska	0.0	0.0	100.0	0.0	0.0	100.0
	North	0.3	9.0	90.7	6.7	33.8	59.5
	Pacific Coast	0.1	3.6	96.3	0.9	9.4	89.7
	Rocky Mountain	0.0	1.2	98.8	0.2	6.0	93.8
	South	0.0	3.6	96.3	1.6	25.9	72.5
	National	0.0	1.6	98.3	0.5	7.9	91.6
118,000 acres	Alaska	0.0	0.0	100.0	0.0	0.0	100.0
	North	0.1	8.7	91.2	6.5	36.9	56.6
	Pacific Coast	0.1	4.3	95.6	0.8	13.1	86.1
	Rocky Mountain	0.0	1.0	98.9	0.1	8.0	91.9
	South	0.0	3.6	96.4	0.9	31.5	67.6
	National	0.0	1.6	98.3	0.3	10.1	89.6

Rows may not add up to 100 due to rounding off the figures.

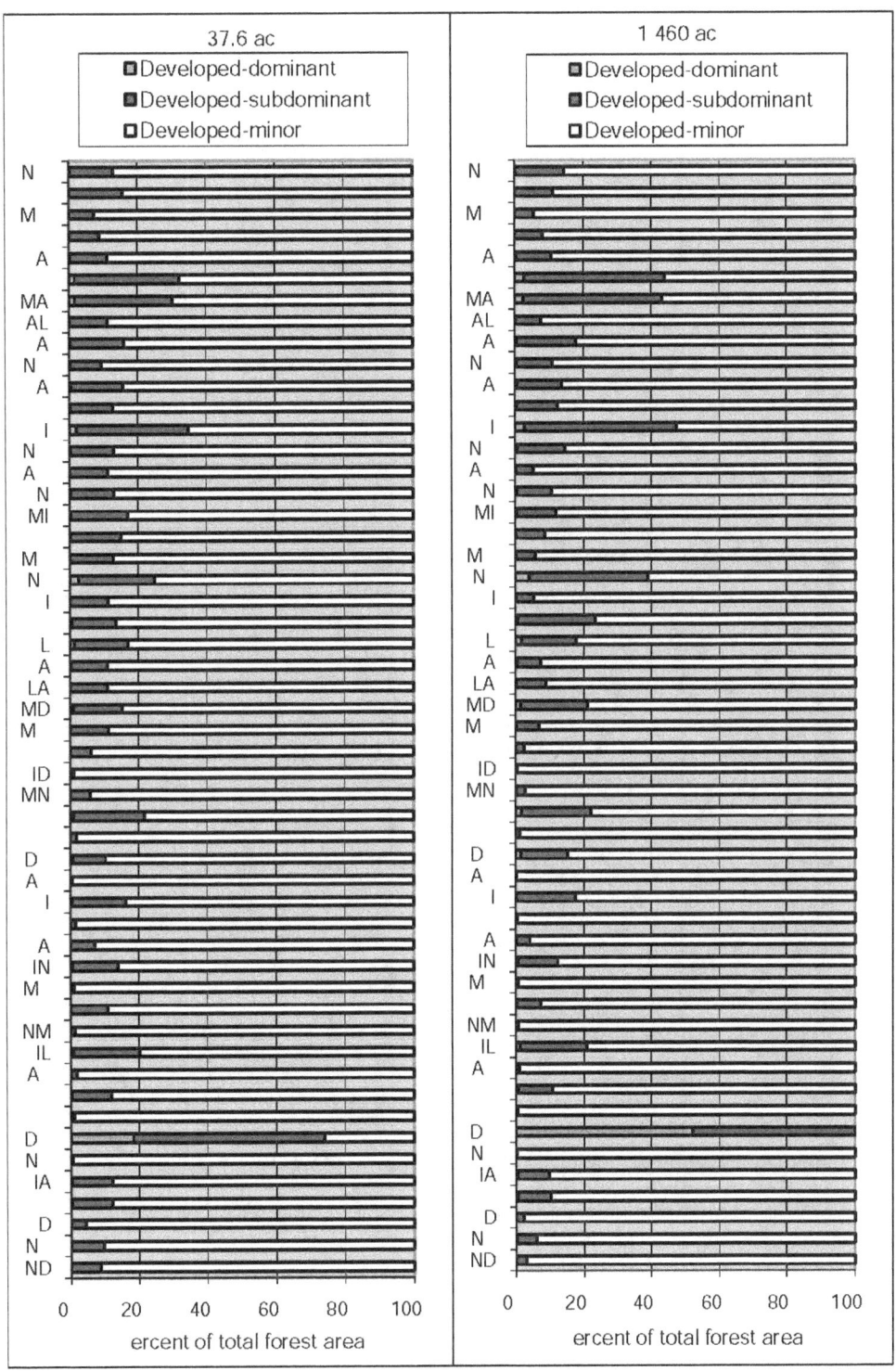

Figure 27—Percent of total forest area in each State in three developed interface zones for neighborhood sizes of 37.6 acres (left) and 1,460 acres (right). States are sorted in descending order by percent forest (fig. 5).

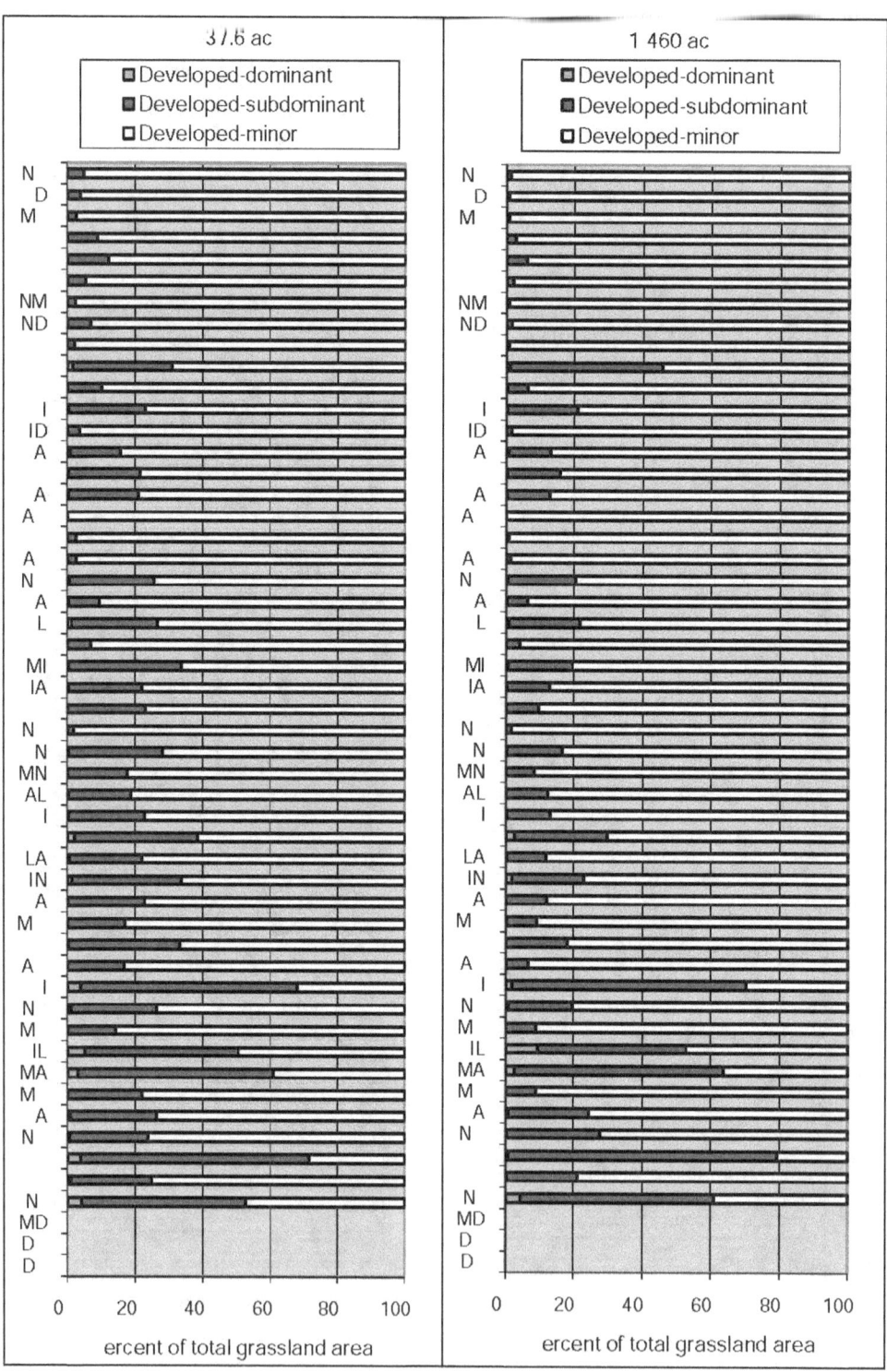

Figure 28—Percent of total grassland area in each State in three developed interface zones for neighborhood sizes of 37.6 acres (left) and 1,460 acres (right). States are sorted in descending order by percent grassland (fig. 5).

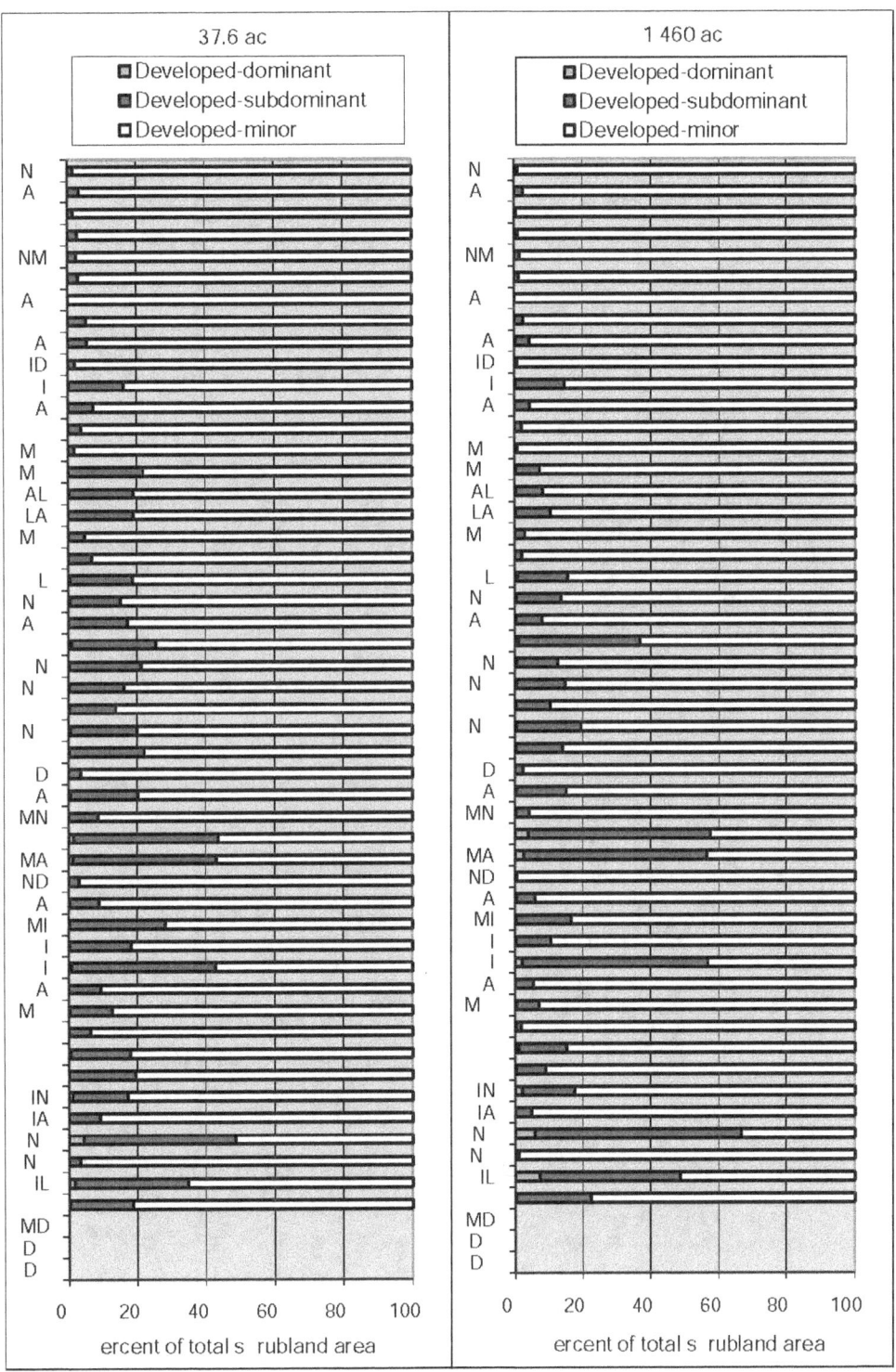

Figure 29—Percent of total shrubland area in each State in three developed interface zones for neighborhood sizes of 37.6 acres (left) and 1,460 acres (right). States are sorted in descending order by percent shrubland (fig. 5).

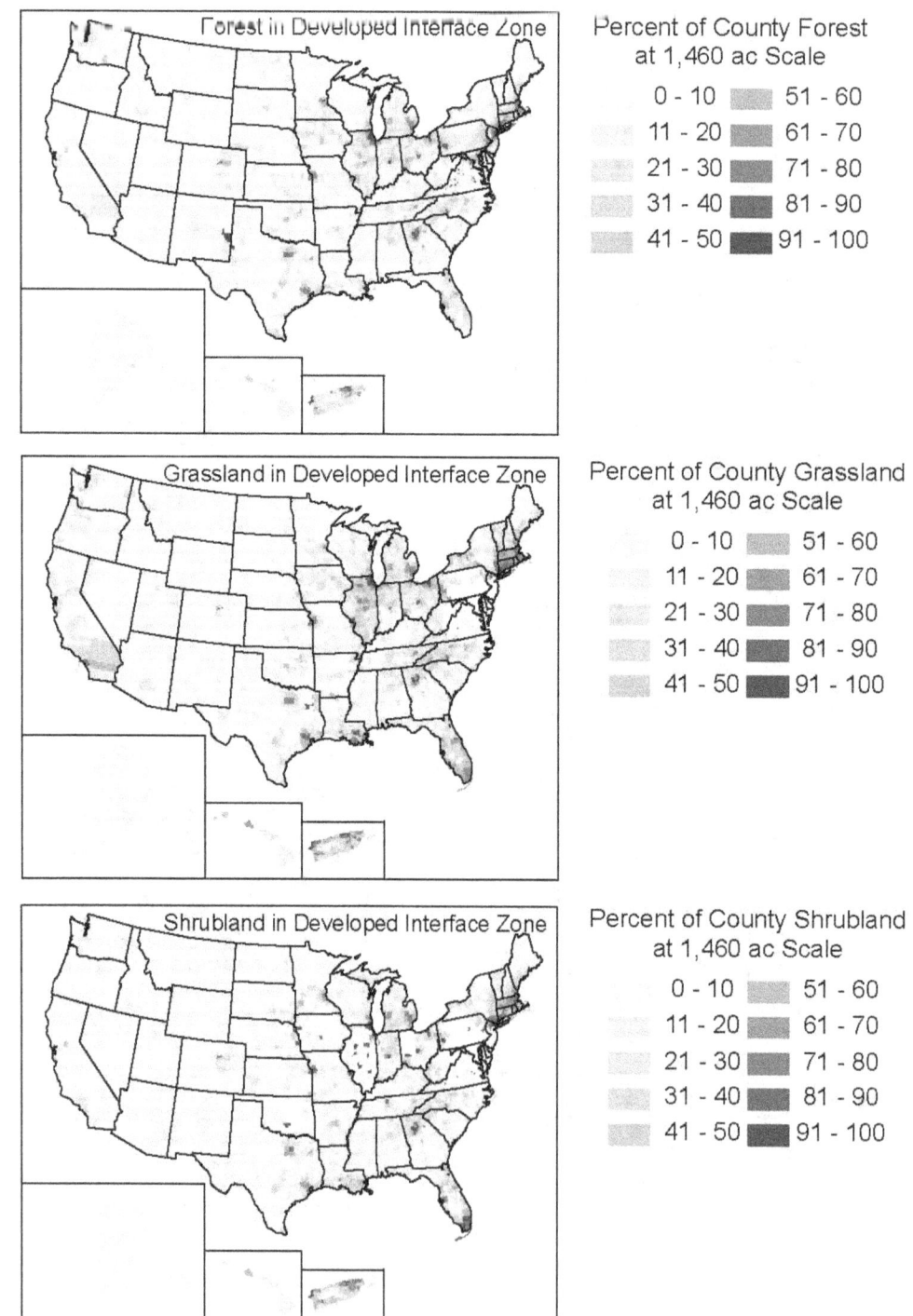

Figure 30—Percent of total county forest (top), grassland (middle), and shrubland (bottom) area in a developed interface zone in 1,460-acre neighborhoods; the developed interface zone includes the developed-dominant and developed-subdominant interface zones.

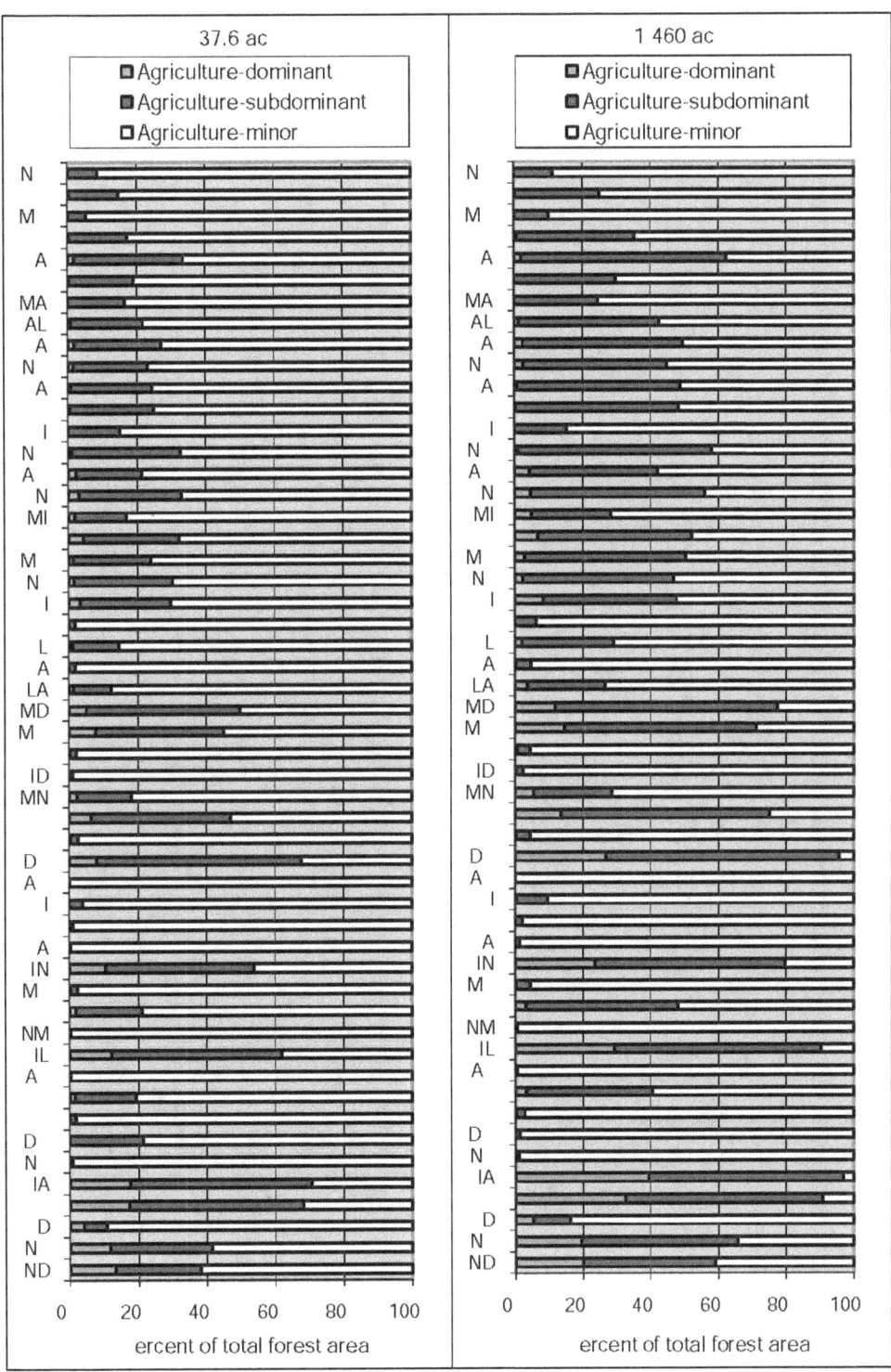

Figure 31—Percent of total forest area in each State in three agriculture interface zones for neighborhood sizes of 37.6 acres (left) and 1,460 acres (right). States are sorted in descending order by percent forest (fig. 5).

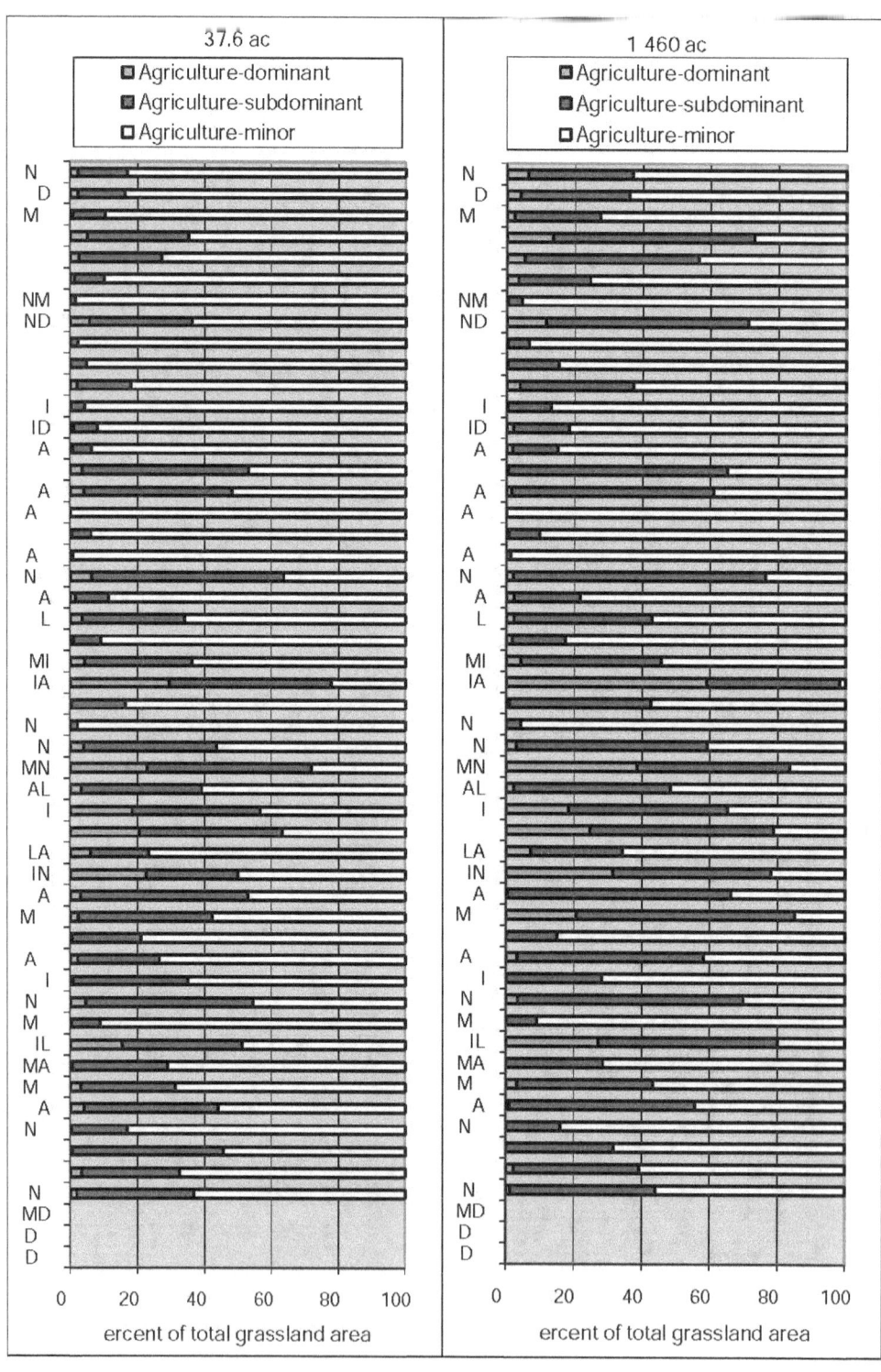

Figure 32—Percent of total grassland area in each State in three agriculture interface zones for neighborhood sizes of 37.6 acres (left) and 1,460 acres (right). States are sorted in descending order by percent grassland (fig. 5).

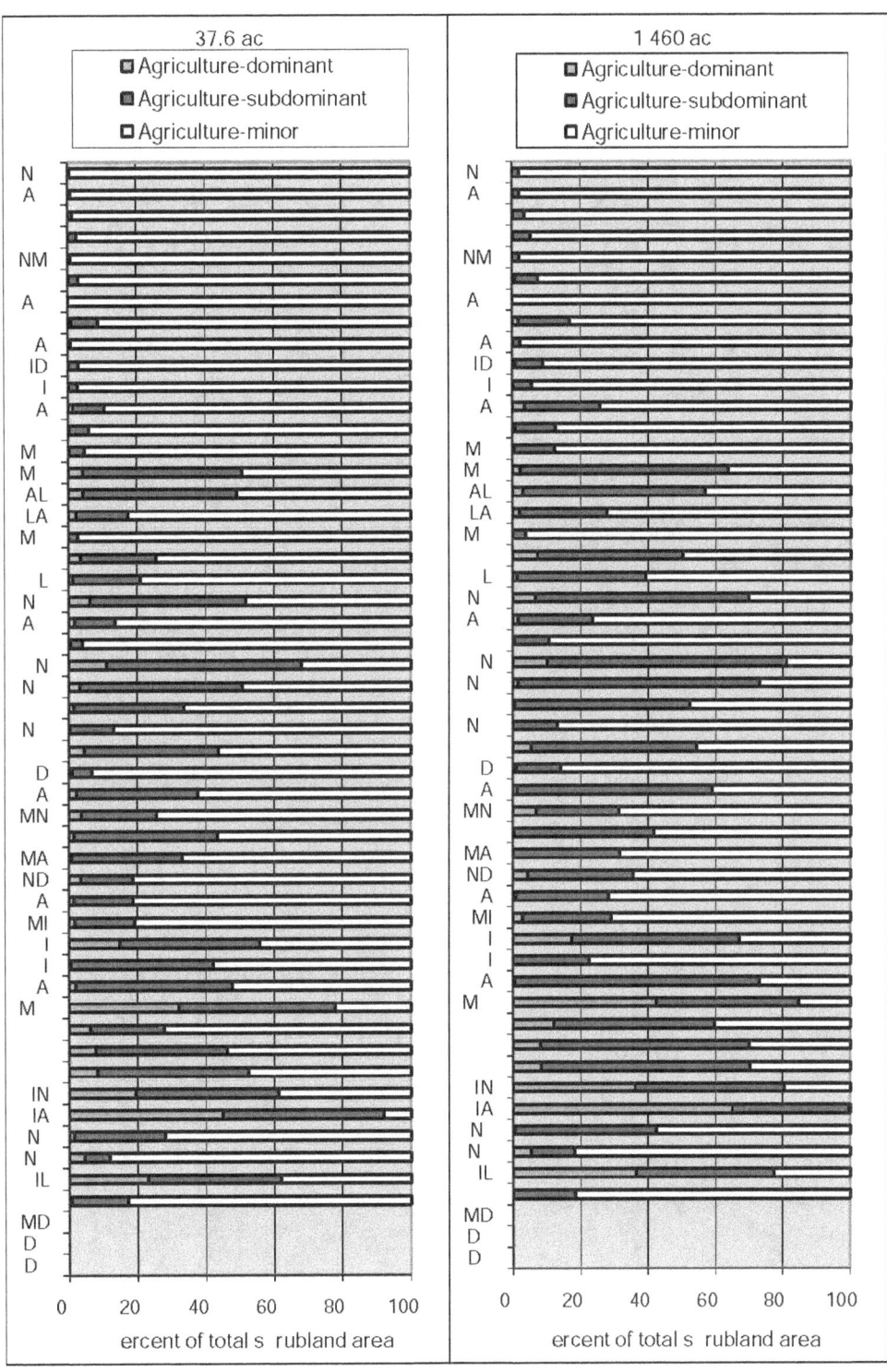

Figure 33—Percent of total shrubland area in each State in three agriculture interface zones for neighborhood sizes of 37.6 acres (left) and 1,460 acres (right). States are sorted in descending order by percent shrubland (fig. 5).

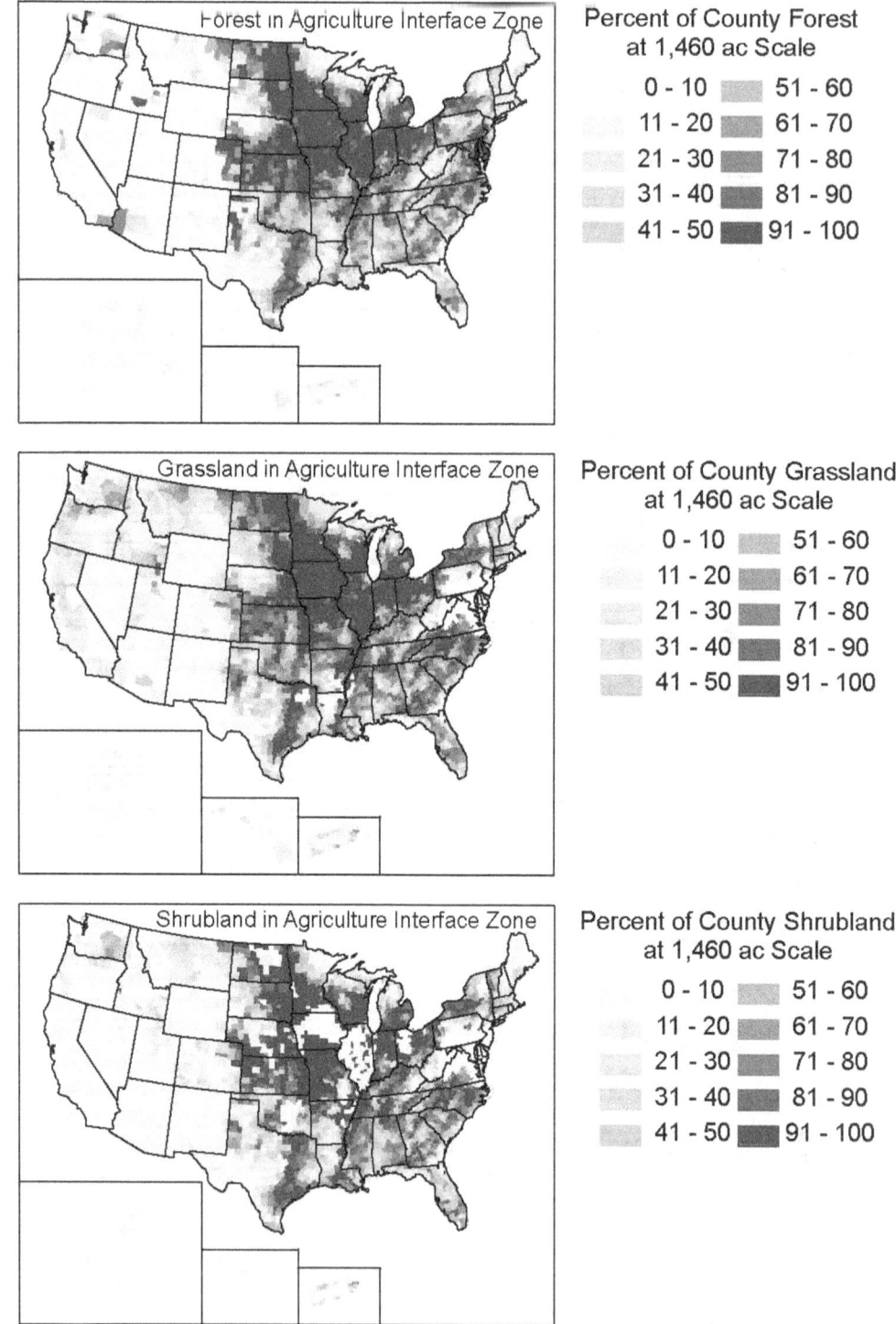

Figure 34—Percent of total county forest (top), grassland (middle), and shrubland (bottom) area in an agriculture interface zone in 1,460-acre neighborhoods; the agriculture interface zone includes the agriculture-dominant and agriculture-subdominant interface zones.

Table 19—Forest structure. Percent of total forest area in six structure classes, for four edge widths, by Forest and Rangeland Renewable Resources Planning Act of 1974 (RPA) region and national

Edge width	Region	Core	Islet	Perforated	Edge	Connector	Branch
				----------Percent----------			
98 feet	Alaska	70.9	3.2	4.9	10.9	6.1	3.8
	North	74.4	1.5	2.7	15.4	2.6	3.4
	Pacific Coast	73.9	1.7	4.9	12.7	3.6	3.3
	Rocky Mountain	71.3	3.5	4.9	12.3	3.7	4.4
	South	71.1	1.8	2.3	17.8	3.1	4.0
	National	72.2	2.2	3.5	14.6	3.6	3.8
197 feet	Alaska	57.6	5.5	5.8	15.4	11.6	4.1
	North	59.0	3.5	3.2	22.6	6.1	5.5
	Pacific Coast	58.8	3.4	5.8	19.1	8.4	4.5
	Rocky Mountain	57.1	6.9	5.7	16.7	8.1	5.6
	South	54.3	4.1	2.1	25.7	7.4	6.4
	National	57.0	4.6	4.0	21.1	7.9	5.5
394 feet	Alaska	45.4	7.2	5.4	19.9	18.6	3.4
	North	44.7	6.5	3.0	27.9	11.7	6.2
	Pacific Coast	44.5	5.1	5.1	25.3	15.8	4.3
	Rocky Mountain	44.4	10.1	5.4	20.8	14.3	5.1
	South	39.1	6.9	1.5	31.1	14.2	7.3
	National	43.0	7.2	3.5	26.2	14.4	5.7
787 feet	Alaska	27.3	10.0	3.4	23.8	33.8	1.7
	North	24.2	13.6	1.6	29.9	26.7	3.9
	Pacific Coast	23.6	7.9	2.1	29.1	35.1	2.2
	Rocky Mountain	26.0	14.7	3.1	24.4	29.3	2.6
	South	18.9	13.2	0.6	29.9	32.5	4.9
	National	23.3	12.6	1.9	27.9	30.9	3.5

Rows may not add up to 100 due to rounding off the figures.

Table 20—Grassland structure. Percent of total grassland area in six structure classes, for four edge widths, by Forest and Rangeland Renewable Resources Planning Act of 1974 (RPA) region and national

Edge width	Region	Core	Islet	Perforated	Edge	Connector	Branch
				Percent			
98 feet	Alaska	46.3	12.2	3.5	18.0	12.0	8.0
	North	18.9	34.2	0.1	24.1	7.9	14.8
	Pacific Coast	50.1	9.3	1.6	22.6	8.0	8.4
	Rocky Mountain	68.7	4.1	2.6	14.1	5.9	4.5
	South	47.8	12.4	1.3	22.1	8.0	8.5
	National	60.4	7.5	2.3	16.7	7.0	6.1
197 feet	Alaska	30.7	20.5	2.7	20.0	19.2	7.0
	North	6.5	62.4	0.0	14.0	7.8	9.2
	Pacific Coast	33.2	18.7	1.3	23.4	14.7	8.7
	Rocky Mountain	55.4	7.6	2.9	18.4	10.8	4.9
	South	31.5	22.4	1.2	23.2	13.4	8.4
	National	46.2	13.6	2.4	19.6	12.2	6.1
394 feet	Alaska	19.8	27.3	1.6	20.1	26.3	4.9
	North	2.1	81.1	0.0	7.0	6.1	3.8
	Pacific Coast	22.1	27.9	0.9	21.5	21.5	6.2
	Rocky Mountain	43.6	10.9	2.8	21.7	16.7	4.4
	South	20.0	31.8	0.8	21.8	18.8	6.7
	National	34.7	19.1	2.1	21.2	17.9	5.0
787 feet	Alaska	8.4	37.6	0.7	14.5	36.9	1.9
	North	0.3	94.8	0.0	1.6	2.8	0.5
	Pacific Coast	10.7	42.2	0.5	15.2	29.4	2.1
	Rocky Mountain	27.2	16.9	2.3	22.9	28.2	2.5
	South	8.7	46.3	0.4	15.1	26.7	2.8
	National	20.4	27.7	1.7	19.7	28.1	2.4

Rows may not add up to 100 due to rounding off the figures.

Table 21—Shrubland structure. Percent of total shrubland area in six structure classes, for four edge widths, by Forest and Rangeland Renewable Resources Planning Act of 1974 (RPA) region and national

Edge width	Region	Core	Islet	Perforated	Edge	Connector	Branch
				----------Percent----------			
98 feet	Alaska	69.2	2.8	5.1	12.0	6.9	4.0
	North	16.9	41.7	0.2	20.7	7.4	13.1
	Pacific Coast	72.8	3.6	2.2	12.1	5.0	4.4
	Rocky Mountain	73.7	3.0	3.3	10.4	5.8	3.8
	South	63.0	8.5	2.6	13.7	6.7	5.6
	National	70.3	4.2	3.5	11.6	6.1	4.3
197 feet	Alaska	54.9	5.0	5.7	16.8	13.1	4.5
	North	6.2	66.4	0.1	12.2	7.9	7.2
	Pacific Coast	62.1	7.7	2.6	13.4	9.5	4.6
	Rocky Mountain	63.1	5.8	3.8	12.3	11.0	4.0
	South	51.2	14.7	3.1	14.5	11.7	5.0
	National	58.5	7.6	4.0	14.0	11.4	4.4
394 feet	Alaska	42.3	6.9	5.1	20.9	21.0	3.7
	North	2.2	79.0	0.0	7.3	7.8	3.7
	Pacific Coast	54.0	11.9	3.0	13.7	14.1	3.4
	Rocky Mountain	54.5	8.3	4.0	13.5	16.7	3.0
	South	42.3	20.0	3.2	14.5	16.6	3.4
	National	48.9	10.7	4.0	15.6	17.4	3.3
787 feet	Alaska	24.4	10.2	3.1	23.2	37.4	1.7
	North	0.2	92.8	0.0	1.5	4.8	0.6
	Pacific Coast	42.8	18.2	3.4	13.5	20.8	1.4
	Rocky Mountain	42.3	12.3	3.8	14.5	25.9	1.3
	South	31.1	26.9	3.3	12.9	24.6	1.2
	National	35.5	15.3	3.4	16.4	28.0	1.4

Rows may not add up to 100 due to rounding off the figures.

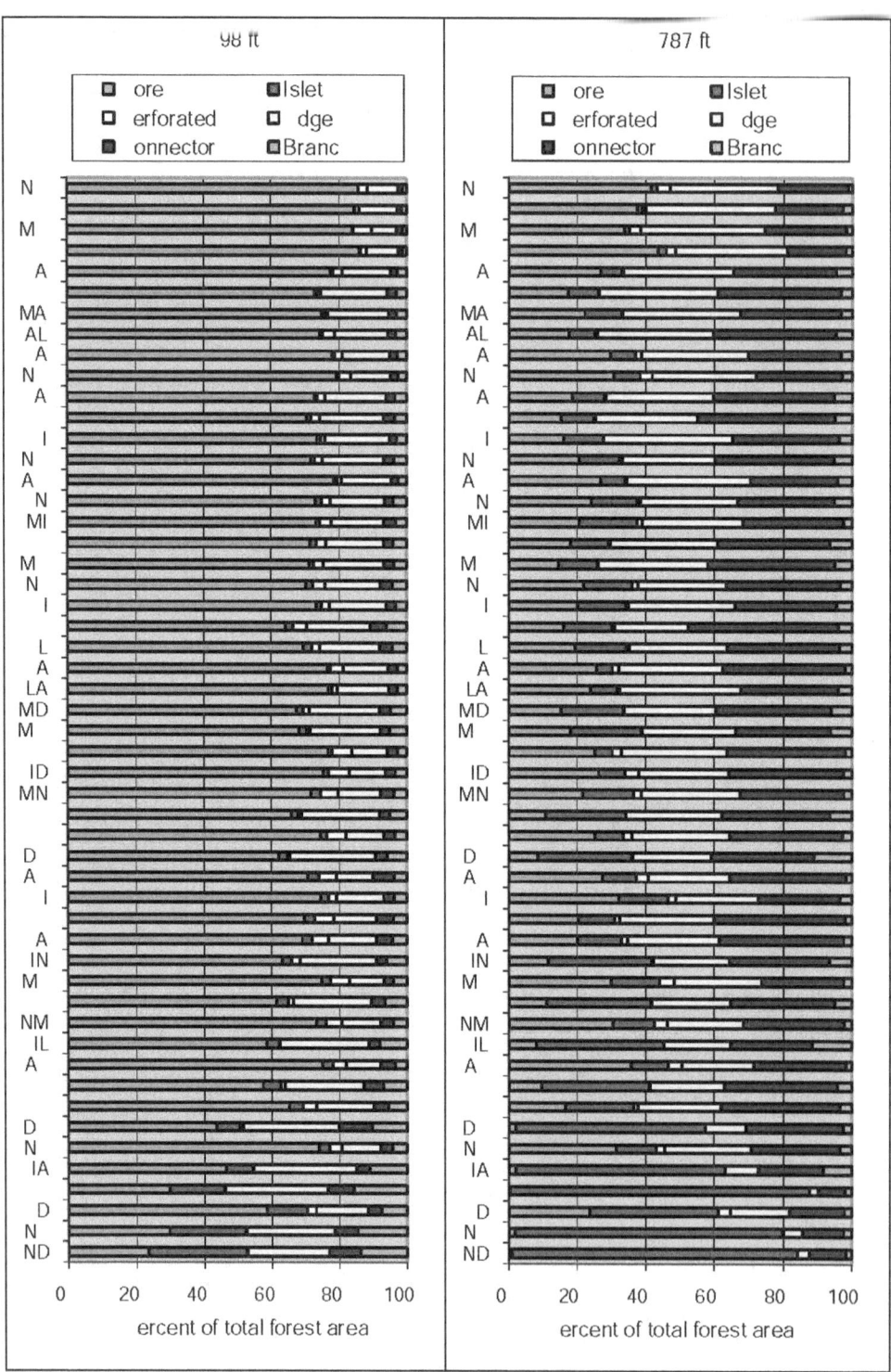

Figure 35—Percent of total forest area in each State in six structure classes for edge widths of 98 feet (left) and 787 feet (right). States are sorted in descending order by percent forest (fig. 5).

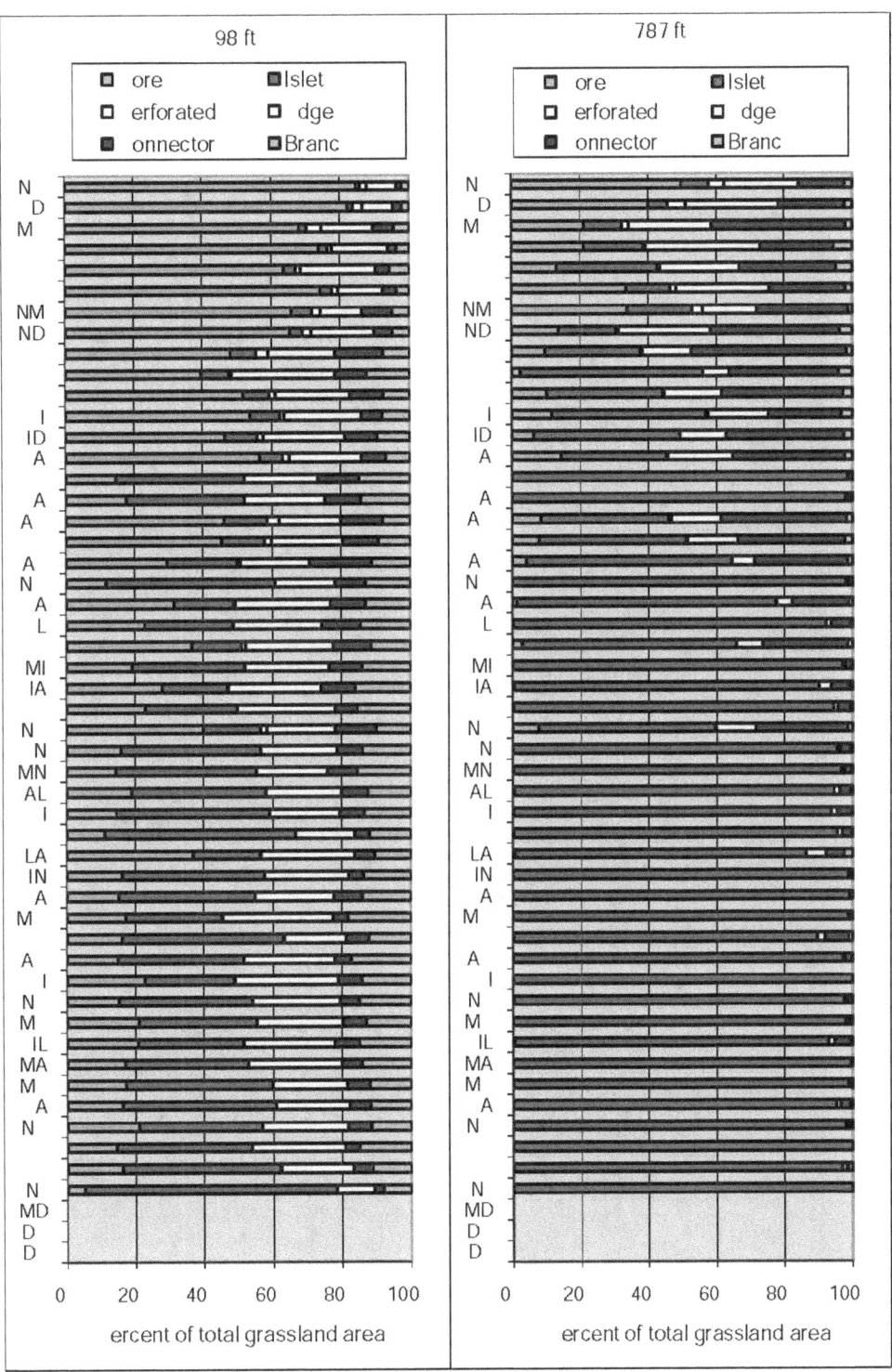

Figure 36—Percent of total grassland area in each State in six structure classes for edge widths of 98 feet (left) and 787 feet (right). States are sorted in descending order by percent grassland (fig. 5).

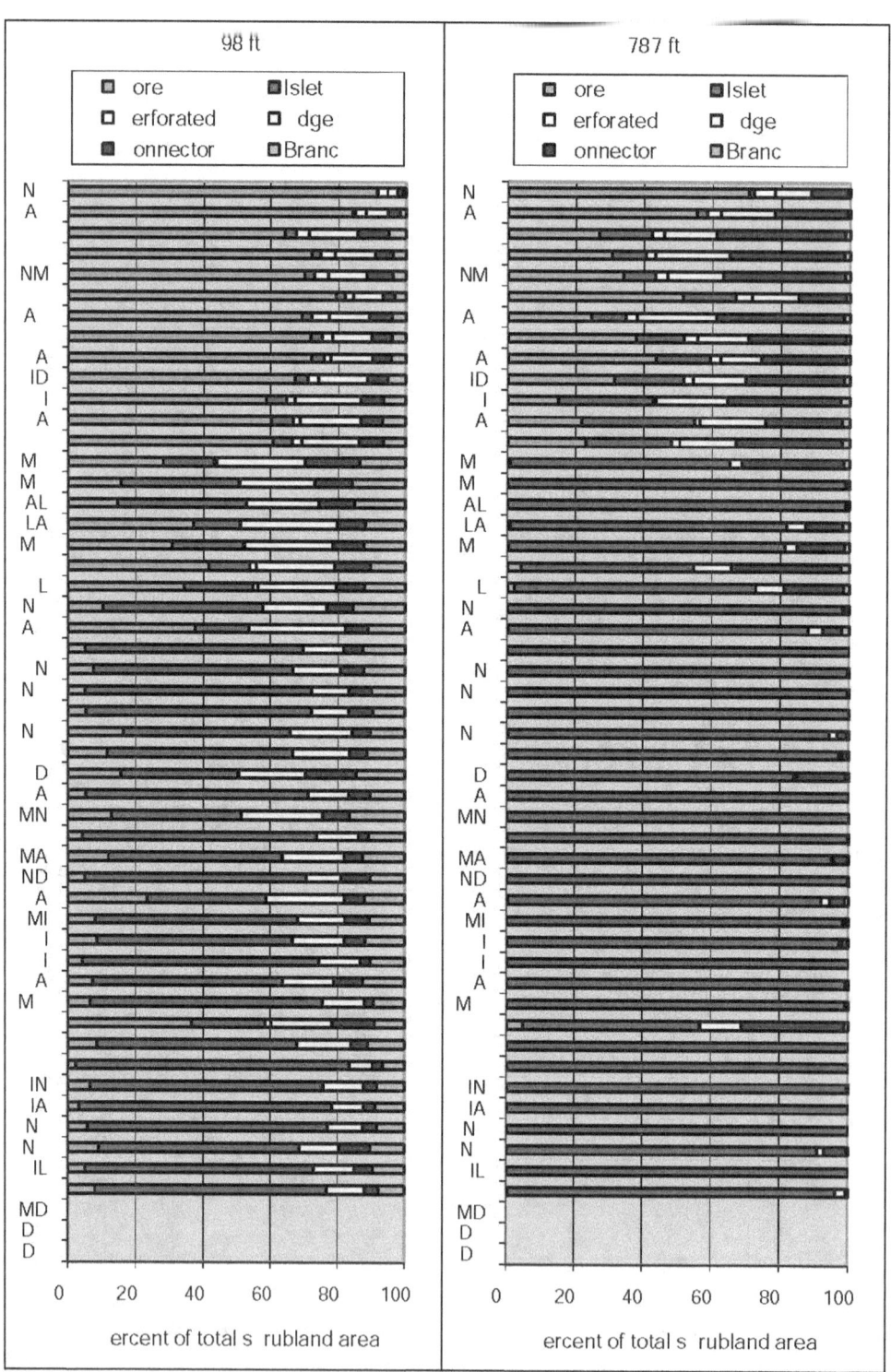

Figure 37—Percent of total shrubland area in each State in six structure classes for edge widths of 98 feet (left) and 787 feet (right). States are sorted in descending order by percent shrubland (fig. 5).

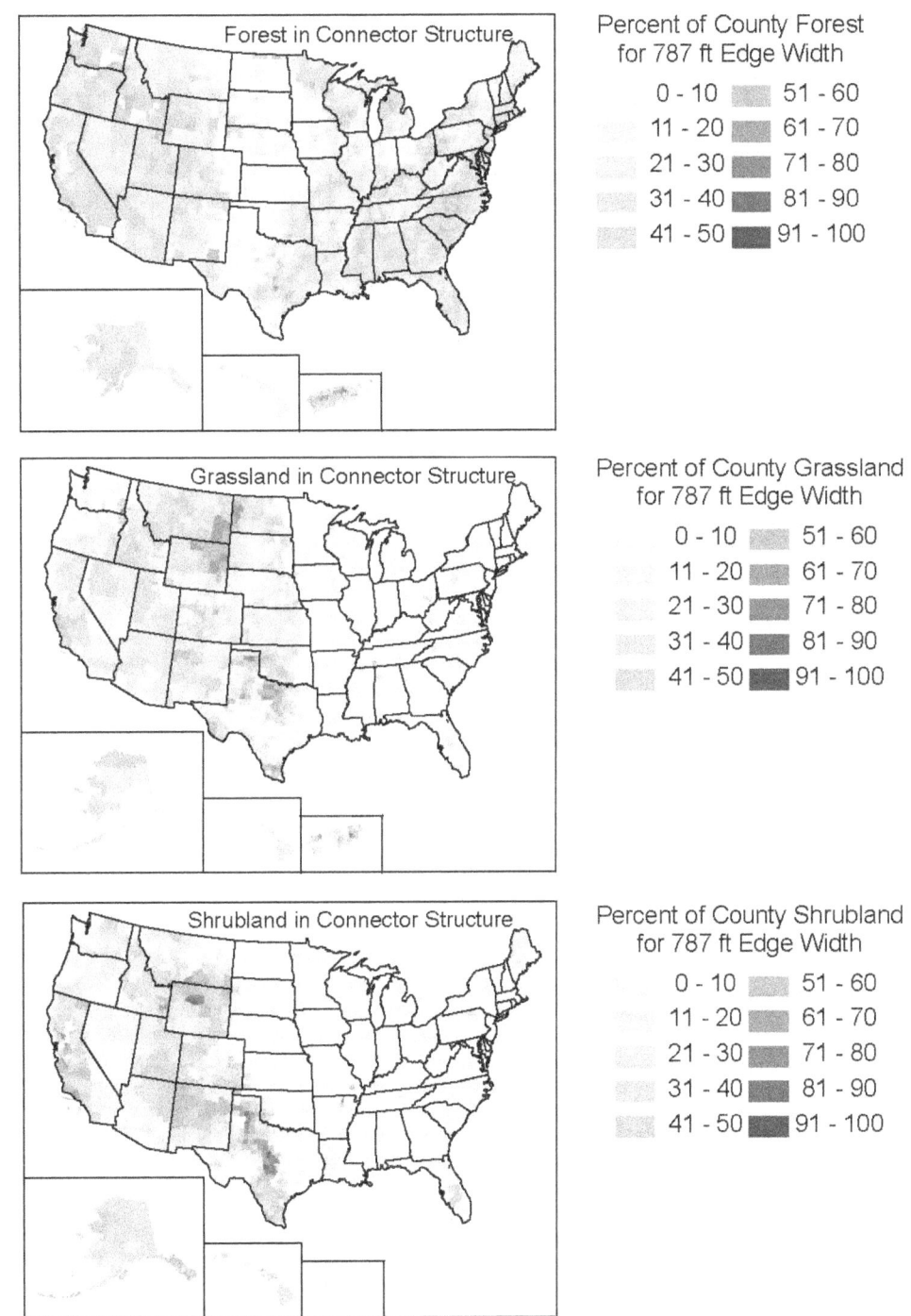

Figure 38—Percent of total county forest (top), grassland (middle), and shrubland (bottom) area in the connector structure class for a 787-foot edge width.

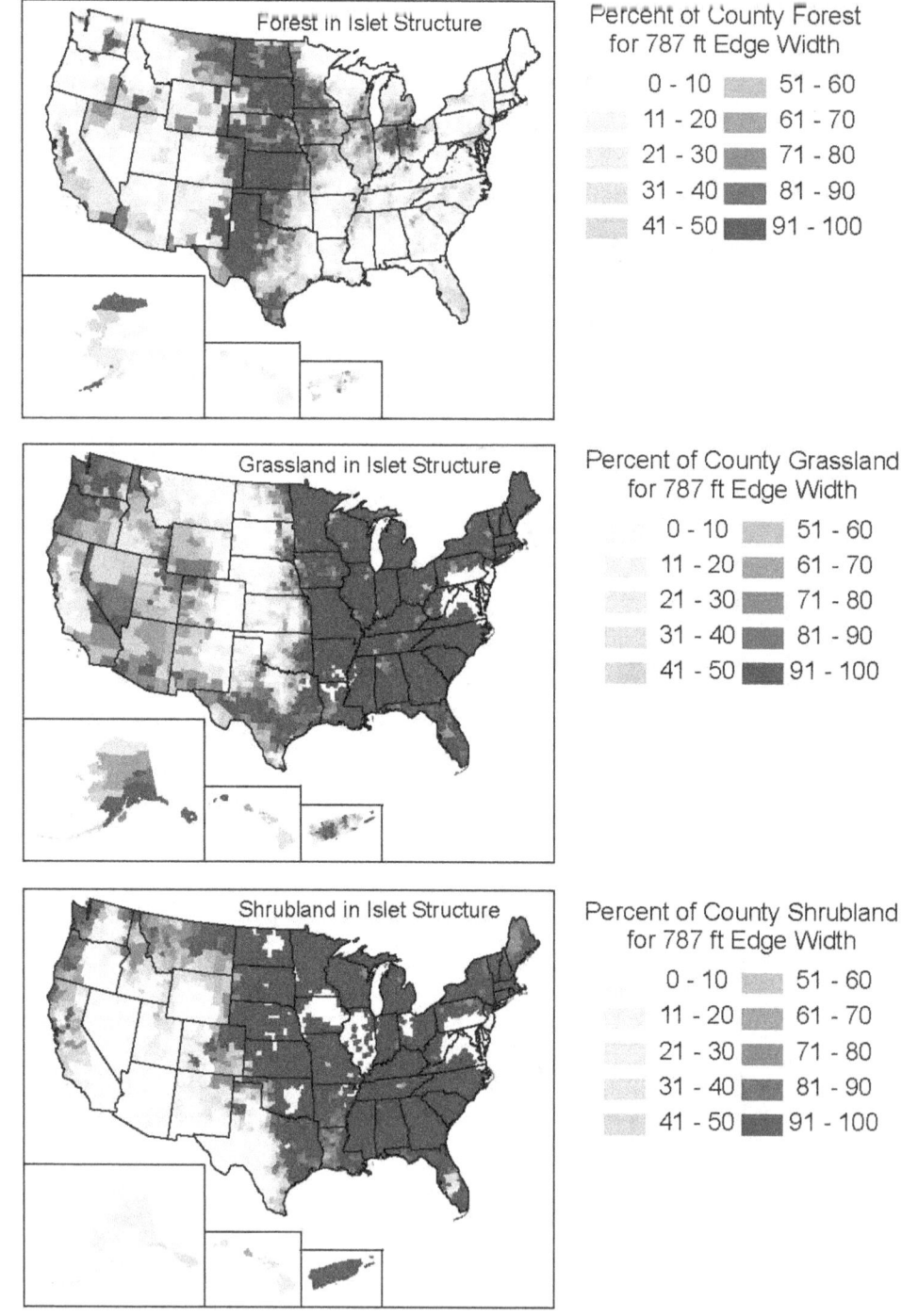

Figure 39—Percent of total county forest (top), grassland (middle), and shrubland (bottom) area in the islet structure class for a 787-foot edge width.

SUMMARY

This report was prepared in response to the requirement for an inventory of land cover spatial patterns in support of the 2010 RPA Assessment. The inventory provides information to help address the sustainability of a wide range of social and ecological amenities that are derived from forest, grassland, and shrubland in the United States. The inventory methods are designed to be generic and extensible, and suitable for application with only a national land cover map at several measurement scales. This report documents the inventory procedures, and presents national and regional summaries of land cover pattern statistics along with illustrative figures and maps showing State and county results. Additional information is available online at http://www.forestthreats.org.

LITERATURE CITED

Bogaert, J. 2003. Lack of agreement on fragmentation metrics blurs correspondence between fragmentation experiments and predicted effects. Ecology and Society. 7(1): r6. http://ecologyandsociety.org/vol7/iss1/resp6. [Date accessed: November 15, 2010].

Burkhard, B.; Kroll, F.; Muller, F.; Windhorst, W. 2009. Landscapes' capacities to provide ecosystem services—a concept for land cover based assessments. Landscape Online. 15: 1-22.

ESRI. 2005. ESRI Data & Maps 2005 [DVD]. Redlands, CA: Environmental Systems Research Institute.

Gee, G.W.; Bauder, J.W. 1986. Particle size analysis. In: Klute, A., ed. Methods of Soil Analysis, Part 1, Physical and Mineralogical Methods. Second Edition. Agronomy Monograph No. 9. Madison, WI: American Society of Agronomy: 383-411.

Heilman, G.E.; Strittholt, J.R.; Slosser, N.C.; Dellasala, D.A. 2002. Forest fragmentation of the conterminous United States: assessing forest intactness through road density and spatial characteristics. BioScience. 52: 411-422.

Homer, C.; Dewitz, J.; Fry, J. [and others]. 2007. Completion of the 2001 national land cover database for the conterminous United States. Photogrammetric Engineering and Remote Sensing. 73: 337-341.

Homer, C.; Huang, C.; Yang, L. [and others]. 2004. Development of a 2001 national land cover database for the United States. Photogrammetric Engineering and Remote Sensing. 70: 829-840.

O'Neill, R.V.; Hunsaker, C.T.; Jones, K.B. [and others]. 1997. Monitoring environmental quality at the landscape scale. BioScience. 47: 513-519.

Ostapowicz, K.; Vogt, P.; Riitters, K.H. [and others]. 2008. Impact of scale on morphological spatial pattern of forest. Landscape Ecology. 23: 1107-1117.

Radeloff, V.C.; Hammer, R.B.; Stewart, S.I. [and others]. 2005. The wildland-urban interface in the United States. Ecological Applications. 15: 799-805.

Riitters, K. 2005. Downscaling indicators of forest habitat structure from national assessments. Ecological Indicators. 5: 273-279.

Riitters, K.H.; Coulston, J.W. 2005. Hot spots of perforated forest in the Eastern United States. Environmental Management. 35: 483-492.

Riitters, K.H.; Coulston, J.W.; Wickham, J.D. 2003. Localizing national fragmentation statistics with forest type maps. Journal of Forestry. 101: 18-22.

Riitters, K.H.; Wickham, J.D. 2003. How far to the nearest road? Frontiers in Ecology and Environment. 1: 125-129.

Riitters, K.H.; Wickham, J.; Coulston, J. 2004a. Use of road maps in national assessments of forest fragmentation in the United States. Ecology and Society. 9(2): 13. http://www.ecologyandsociety.org/vol9/iss2/art13. [Date accessed: November 15, 2010].

Riitters, K.H.; Wickham, J.D.; Coulston, J.W. 2004b. A preliminary assessment of Montreal Process indicators of forest fragmentation for the United States. Environmental Monitoring and Assessment. 91: 257-276.

Riitters, K.H.; Wickham, J.D.; O'Neill, R.V. [and others]. 2002. Fragmentation of continental United States forests. Ecosystems. 5: 815-822.

Riitters, K.H.; Wickham, J.D.; Vogelmann, J.E.; Jones, K.B. 2000. National land cover pattern data. Ecology. 81: 604-608.

Riitters, K.H.; Vogt, P.; Soille, P. [and others]. 2007. Neutral model analysis of landscape patterns from mathematical morphology. Landscape Ecology. 22: 1033-1044.

Riitters, K.H.; Wickham, J.D.; Wade, T.G. 2009a. An indicator of forest dynamics using a shifting landscape mosaic. Ecological Indicators. 9: 107-117.

Riitters, K.H.; Wickham, J.D.; Wade, T.G. 2009b. Evaluating anthropogenic risk of grassland and forest habitat degradation using land cover data. Landscape Online. 13: 1-14.

Soille, P.; Vogt, P. 2009. Morphological segmentation of binary patterns. Pattern Recognition Letters. 30: 456-459.

Stewart, S.I.; Radeloff, V.C.; Hammer, R.B.; Hawbaker, T.J. 2007. Defining the wildland-urban interface. Journal of Forestry. 105: 201-207.

Vogt, P.; Riitters, K.H.; Estreguil, C. [and others]. 2007a. Mapping spatial patterns with morphological image processing. Landscape Ecology. 22: 171-177.

Vogt, P.; Riitters, K.H.; Iwanowski, M. [and others]. 2007b. Mapping landscape corridors. Ecological Indicators. 7: 481-488.

Wade, T. 2004. Causes of forest fragmentation in the United States – 270 meter resolution. National Atlas of the United States. Reston, VA: http://www.nationalatlas.gov/metadata/frfrg2i270l.faq.html. [Date accessed: November 15, 2010].

Wade, T.G.; Riitters, K.H.; Wickham, J.D.; Jones, K.B. 2003. Distribution and causes of global forest fragmentation. Ecology and Society. 7(2): 7. http://www.ecologyandsociety.org/vol7/iss2/art7. [Date accessed: November 15, 2010].

Wickham, J.D.; Riitters, K.H.; Wade, T.G.; Homer, C. 2008. Temporal change in fragmentation of continental U.S. forests. Landscape Ecology. 23: 891-898.

Wickham, J.D.; Stehman, S.V.; Fry, J.A. [and others]. 2010. Thematic accuracy of the NLCD 2001 land cover for the conterminous United States. Remote Sensing of Environment. 114: 1286-1296.

Zurlini, G.; Riitters, K.H.; Zaccarelli, N.; Petrosillo, I. 2007. Patterns of disturbance at multiple scales in real and simulated landscapes. Landscape Ecology. 22: 705-721.

www.ingramcontent.com/pod-product-compliance
Lightning Source LLC
Chambersburg PA
CBHW081239280526
45787CB00006B/2726